I WANT TO BE METRO POLITAN

TO BE

BOSTON CASE STUDY

ORO

CONTENTS

42°21' 28" N
71°03' 42" W

MINI METRO POLITAN- ISM

BY: DONGWOO YIM

As Rem Koolhaas has insisted, urbanism has died already. With the con-tinuous and rigorous growth of cities, not only in terms of their size but also of their number, more than half of the planet's population live in cities. More than 75% are expected to live in cities by 2050. Then shouldn't the discourse on urbanism be more viable and stronger than ever with this radical growth of cities? Perhaps the death of urbanism comes from the fact that nowadays most of living areas are urban, and thus, anything can be urbanism – just as there would not be a concept of super car if all cars are super car. That said, the concept of urbanism shouldn't be confined by our traditional means of counting urbanized areas and mega-cities. In fact, since post-modernism, various urbanisms have been emerged and discussed. From Rem Koolhaas' unique perspective on New York to Jane Jacob's influential perspective on American cities, and from urbanisms on traditional European cities to emerging urbanisms of fast-growing Asian cities, the number of urbanisms have emerged to read, analyze, and fore-see the city.

However though, it is true that most of urbanisms these days deal with very extreme conditions such as density, informality, congestion, expeditious growth or shrinking and so on. It is mostly because of the nature of urbanism. Because of radical transformation of cities since the industrial era, urbanism always emerged to 'solve' problems in a city as a result of the radical transition and extreme conditions. For instance, Garden City movement emerged to propose alternative to industrial cities then with congestion and pollution, and Le Corbusier's idea in Plan de Voisin was dealing with increasing density of city. And thus, in nature, urbanism has a perspective of dealing with urban 'troubles', no matter whether it is to solve or face the trouble. However, we all may agree that urbanism is not just about extreme urban conditions. As mentioned above, there are so many different types of urban setting, which are not always extreme, and urbanism cannot just focus on certain types of settings. But at the same time, we may admit that many urbanisms we know currently are mostly

IT IS TRUE THAT MOST OF URBANISMS THESE DAYS DEAL WITH VERY EXTREME CONDITIONS SUCH AS DENSITY, INFORMALITY, CONGESTION, EXPEDITIOUS GROWTH OR SHRINKING AND SO ON

"

dealing with extreme conditions. Then what happens to other cities that do not seem to have extreme settings? Perhaps, there are more numbers of cities in the world that are not as dense as New York City, not as fast-growing as Shanghai, or not as congested as Mumbai. What can we see from those 'less' extreme setting cities? And what perspective can be taken into account?

Among the less extreme cities, our concept of MINI Metropolitanism focuses on city that is conceived as a metropolis in a broader sense of the definition, which is not necessarily a metropolis in the strictest sense of the term. In fact, defining what is a metropolis or metropolitan is not easy at all, let alone MINI Metropolis. It is because, after all, in many cases, the definition ends up being very subjective. According to the Oxford Dictionary, the word "metropolis" simply means "a very large and busy city." Hardly would people argue against the idea that New York City is a metropolis or metropolitan. Yet, arguments arise when we say that a smaller, less dominating in the global corporate business circuit city like Milano is a metropolis or metropolitan. Some people would say it is neither metropolis nor metropolitan, while others may say it is metropolitan but not a metropolis, and still some others will say Milano is a metropolis. Mostly, the argument comes from the fact that a city is different from New York – the de jure model of a metropolis. As mentioned, there is little argument about mega-metropolis being a metropolis. However, as some people understand metropolis as a 'mega-city' while some conceive as an 'urbanized city', cities that are not categorized as mega-metropolis are pretty much arguable.

Perhaps, the confusion comes from the traditional concept of metropolis. When bigger cities started to emerge since the industrialization era, there was a clear hierarchy between the rural, city and metropolis. A metropolis was a larger city where not only manufacturing industries gathers but also all different types of urban activities, such as consumption, education and cultural exchange happened in regional scale. This was the moment when the concept of mega-metropolis or global city was yet to invented. However, nowadays, urban activities in a metropolis are not confined in the regional, but go beyond the global level. There is no border between nations in financial trade any more and students are moving around the whole world for education. This is the moment when mega-metropolis, such as New York and London, emerges in global scale, and thus, cities that are not mega-metropolis became arguable to be metropolis or metropolitan. Here, we are not trying to objectively define what is metropolis or not, instead, we will focus on metropolitan aspects in a city that is not conceived as mega-metropolis.

Then what type of cities that we are focusing on in our concept of MINI

Metropolitanism? As we may imagine from the term itself, it is, for sure, not about mega-metropolis. In the book "Metropolitan World Atlas," they picked hundred and one cities as metropolitan cities. Among more than hundred cities there are only several mega-metropolises, such as London, Tokyo, and New York. Perhaps the rest of the cities, 80-90 of them, have potentials to be MINI Metropolis. However, we would like to narrow it down more clearly with certain characteristics in urbanism. Although cities like London, Tokyo and New York, which we call dense mega-metropolis, or cities like Shanghai and Seoul, which are fastest-growing cities, or cities like Mumbai, Lagos and Caracas, which are cities of congestion, may provide us more stimulating topic in urbanism, still cities like Seattle, Amsterdam, Copenhagen, Tai Pei, San Francisco, Toronto or Barcelona also give us interesting and important issues we have to address in the period of flow of urbanisms. Although it is not so easy to come up with a word that can explain urban conditions of these cities, unlike 'density' for New York, 'congestion' for Caracas, or 'fast' for Shanghai, they share certain characters such as, medium density, established infrastructure, and gradual growth.

With 585,000 inhabitants, Düsseldorf, strictly speaking, is not really a metropolis but it is located in the middle of Germany's most populous and most densely settled urban region, the Rhein-Ruhr where 10 million people live. The population of Düsseldorf, the state capital, is constantly growing thanks to the relatively high – for a small city – numbers of newcomers from the rest of Germany and around the world.

-"New to Dusseldorf-the mini metropolis" New in the City

Often because of the comparison with mega-metropolis, a MINI Metropolis is misunderstood as second tier city. It may be true that a MINI Metropolis does not have as many influential aspects as mega-metropolis in over all, however though, it still has to be distinguished from cities that have all

"

MINI METROPOLIS IS FAR FROM UNDER-DEVELOPMENT. IT IS NOT ABOUT A CITY THAT DOES NOT HAVE A SUFFICIENT QUALITY OF BUILT ENVIRONMENT TO BECOME A METROPOLIS OR A MEGA-METROPOLIS AS IT GETS DEVELOPED, BUT ABOUT A VERY WELL ESTABLISHED CITY AND ITS CONTINUOUS GROWTH MODEL

aspects in second tier. For instance, Düsseldorf describes itself as a small metropolis that has big things to offer. Although it is not the biggest city in Germany for sure, it still is a core city for fashion and culture. Also Dr. Peter Kurz, the Mayor of Mannheim, also in Germany, defines the city as MINI Metropolis as well with its innovative potentials. And thus, we can say a MINI Metropolis has certain aspects that can put the city in the first tier city in certain categories, and those may be generators that sustains the city and let the city grow gradually, if not fast. And in some aspects, a MINI Metropolis can be referred to as a boutique city in a sense that it has very decent quality of living, just as a boutique hotel has a good quality amenities yet different from international chain hotels. Although mostly a boutique city is explained with its demographics, such as elite groups, in a MINI Metropolis, we would like to focus more on its quality of the built environment.

As we may agree now, MINI Metropolis is far from under-development. It is not about a city that does not have a sufficient quality of built environment to become a metropolis or a mega-metropolis as it gets developed, but about a very well established city and its continuous growth model. Because of its established built environment, there are many aspects that a MINI Metropolis shares with other metropolises and especially with mega-metropolis, which we call "metropolitan aspects". These aspects are features of built environment that emerged by force of metropolitan setting/condition, and thus, may occur often in mega-metropolis, which is why it is called "metropolitan" aspects, and perhaps not that often in a MINI Metropolis, because of its weaker force of being metropolitan. However, these aspects are found in a MINI Metropolis occasionally, if not often, and in MINI Metropolitanism, this metropolitan aspect is the key word in reading a city as well as in picturing its future. It is important because, in many cases and scales, metropolitan aspect occurs along the path of growth and development of a city and it becomes a barometer to understand the perspective of the city then. Furthermore, it can provide us a set of guidelines when we have to picture a growth model for the future. Therefore, when we read those metropolitan aspects in a MINI Metropolis, it is not just about the reading the past but also seeing the potentials for the future.

I WANT TO BE METRO-POLITAN

BY: DONGWOO YIM

How is Boston perceived by the local Bostonians or by people from outside? Are their perceptions of Boston similar? Or are they different? An Interesting thing about Boston is that almost every single person in the world knows or has heard about Boston, but not all of them have a clear idea of how big/or small it is. While some people, who have not been to the city, think Boston is quite big, many think it is just a tiny little city compared to other major international cities. Interestingly, many people who visit Boston for the first time usually plan several days to stay in the city and end up only spending a couple of days to cover most of its touristic attractions. Of course, the city is more than what tourists conceive, but yet it is these touristic perceptions that tell us how big the city is. For instance, it is hard to believe the size of Boston is almost the same as that of the inner ring Paris. Perhaps, it is mostly because the area that we experience as a visitor is so much different between those two cities.

Then is Boston a small city? As a matter of fact, it is still the biggest city in the northeastern part of the United States, and, believe or not, the city of Boston is as dense as the Metropolitan London. Also, as a metropolitan area, Greater Boston is the fifth biggest metropolitan area in the United States with its 7.5 million population, next to New York, Los Angeles, Chicago and Washington metropolitan areas.

Does the fact that Boston has a metropolitan area make it a metropolis? Mostly, like big cities such as Tokyo, the metropolitan Tokyo is not just an administrative boundary but also a physical area where most of urban activities take place dependent from the core of the city of Tokyo. Thus, the more dependent areas the city has, the faster the inner city grows. Eventually, it becomes a metropolis. Metropolis as a definition is a large or important city in its region. But as we see from

14
15

THE TERM "URBANISM" HIGHLIGHTS THE IMPORTANCE OF UNDERSTANDING THE PERSPECTIVE THAT TAKES ITS OWN PATH BY ENGAGING ARCHITECTURE, LANDSCAPE AND INFRASTRUCTURE.

"

---

the example of Tokyo, a metropolis is more than just an important city; it is where all those urban activities and interactions happen. It sometimes even absorbs activities from other areas. Therefore, it is quite questionable to say Boston is a metropolis just because it has sort of designate areas as "metropolitan." And more importantly, no matter what the definition of a metropolis is, many people, whether they have been to Boston or not, would not consider it a metropolis, where as cities like New York, London, Shanghai are and will always been perceived as metropolis.

In fact, Boston is almost a perfect example of, what we call, a MINI Metropolis. A MINI Metropolis is a city that is smaller in size than a mega-metropolis, yet continuously growing due to its strengths in certain fields. Boston is often compared with New York not only in terms of the population's interest in national sports but also in many other aspects, such as rent, gross domestic product, or living expenses. In addition, Boston itself sometimes tries to compete with New York. But more often, Boston is perceived as a second-tier city just because of that comparison to New York, an unquestionable first-tier city and mega-metropolis. It is true that Boston is neither as economically nor culturally influential as New York or London. For instance, we have to see London or New York to foresee upcoming trend for fashion, and we have to observe Wall Street's stock market to analyze other markets in the world. However, we would admit that Boston is not just a second tier city when we go through certain aspects such as institutional influence. As we all know, Boston is most prominent in its educational prestige and biomedical technology and research. Then, Boston is not a conventional second-tier city but a city that has more influence, more potentials and more descent quality that sometimes can be easily compared to a mega-metropolis.

Needless to say, there is a series of discrepancies between those mega-metropolises and Boston in many ways, such as in density, population and type of businesses. However though, interestingly enough, we still can find many features in Boston that are METROPOLITAN. These are features are mostly found only in METROPOLIS and which we can characterize a METROPOLIS with. In fact, METROPOLITAN aspects are found in various scales in Boston through out its history. Although it is not easy to define what exactly METROPOLITAN aspects means, when we see the scale of efforts, character of features and property of projects, we can easily link them to certain characters of a METROPOLIS. For instance, the city of Boston started with 785 acres of land and now it claimed more than 4,000 acres of land by continuous landfill projects throughout history. Also, with having the first public park in the United States, Boston Common, Boston has proceeded one of the largest landscape projects in the nation through Emerald Necklace by the renowned landscape architect Frederic Law Olmsted and Metropolitan Park system by Eliot. Because of their scale, major infrastructural projects like these barely happen in a small scale city, and they mostly happen in a major city, as part of efforts to make the city as METROPOLITAN.

When we look back at the growth of the city of Boston, its population once reached 800,000 in the 1950s with a continuous growth since the 1800s. Its population almost doubled from the 1890s to the 1950s. Now, the city of Boston has around 600,000 people residing in the city, 200,000 thousand less than its maximum point, while the world's population has tripled and the United States' population has doubled since the 1950s. Therefore, we can say that relatively Boston was closer to a METROPOLIS that it is now, and perhaps, this explains backgrounds of lots of METROPOLITAN efforts that the city had made back in those days. Yet, there are still major infrastructural efforts in the city these days as well, and this is why the city is so much interesting to see through eyes of METROPOLITAN.

The Big Dig project and air rights planning vision over Massachusetts Turnpike are examples of Boston's METROPOLITAN aspects that are occurring around the city in present. Besides these large scale infrastructural efforts, there are other efforts that give Boston a character of a METROPOLITAN. For instance, Boston area has the best and the biggest area for biotechnology enterprises in the world in and around Kendall Square in Cambridge, and the Longwood Medical Area in Boston is also one of the best quality medical areas in the world. These features can be explained as urban cores in a way that they attract many people to the areas and serve as a catalyst for urban activities. The concept of urban cores plays a very important role in a city and influences a person's perception of the city. For example, the perception of Boston by sports fans are not the same as that of visitors to Boston for conferences or residing college students. It is because there are many different cores in Boston that attract different groups of people for different reasons, and mostly the perception of a city relies on urban experiences a person had in the urban cores. Therefore, Boston sports fans see the city through the area around the home of Boston Red Sox the Fenway Park or the Boston Celtics' home stadium the TD Garden, while students of Harvard University consider Harvard Square as "Boston."

As we see various means of perceptions based on the characteristics of each urban core, the more depth and layers are there in the city. And this variety of perceptions and urban activities can be considered as METROPOLITAN. There are small-scale cities that have a single core so that most of urban activities are compacted into a certain area, and therefore, the perceptions of the city is very confined and the urban interactions are very limited. And perhaps, considering its size and population, Boston needs not to have this many cores in different areas. However, the fact is that Boston already has multiple cores in a city that resemble the feature of a METROPOLIS. When we think about Tokyo, it is very hard to say which part of the city is the major core, because it has numbers of different cores that pull people into the area. For instance, the Nihonbashi area serves as Tokyo's financial core, while the areas around Shinjuku Station serves as the transportation hub and commercial core. Same thing goes on to cultural cores, athletic cores and industrial cores. Although the scale of these cores are so much larger than the ones in Boston, perhaps it is the fact that Boston has multiple urban cores like any other METROPOLISES that gives the city a unique identity and the METROPOLITAN aspects. Boston's multiple urban cores are not just results of its long history. Similar to the large-scale infrastructural efforts in the city, those cores are the present and many of them are growing bigger and bigger, and addition to current multiple cores, Boston is expected to have more cores in the near future. For instance, recently, more world class biotechnology companies are being established in Kendall Square, and Innovation District in South Boston and Harvard Allston campus are expected to be the catalyst of more various industries in the city. They all have the potential to become new urban cores in Boston eventually.

EMPLOYING THE PERSPECTIVE OF INTEGRAL URBANISM WHILE READING BOSTON DOES NOT INTEND TO SKETCH AN ALIEN MASTER PLAN FOR THE FUTURE. RATHER, IT STRIVES TO UNDERSTAND THE EXISTING ECONOMY, CULTURE, AND SOCIETY BETTER AND FORESEE HOW A NEW FLOW OF DEMANDS CAN ACCOMMODATE THEM.

"

As mentioned above, METROPOLITAN aspects are found in various scales in Boston, and they can also be found in smaller scale like architectural projects. Just as efforts in other scales, in architecture scale, it is not easy to define what could be understood as METROPOLITAN architecture. The reason why understanding METROPOLITAN architecture is important is not because Office for Metropolitan Architecture (OMA) has become in the doctrine of architecture but because it is a way of understanding the city. As Fenton argued, a hybrid building is a barometer of our society's evolution process, and here, we understand a hybrid building as METROPOLITAN architecture. Hybrid buildings emerge to accommodate denser urban conditions, various urban demands, and restricted environments, which are also personalities of METROPOLIS. Hybrid building is different from a mixed-use building, which means we are not seeing a project as METROPOLITAN architecture just because it is used for multiple purposes. Mixed-use buildings emerge almost any where in any conditions. For instance, it is not hard to find a condominium on top of retail stores on ground even in Austin, Texas. They emerge because of the convenience of mixed-use not because of the extreme urban setting. And that is why we see so many hybrid buildings in a METROPOLIS where urban conditions go very extreme. The book "Made in Tokyo" by Atlier Bow-Wow, shows us so many buildings, which are architectures without architects, that just happened to emerge in an extreme urban condition of Tokyo. For instance, a temple is located on top of parking garage, and housing units are residing under an elevated rail way. When we see these projects, they look very interesting because of their unique ways of dealing with extreme conditions, but in most of cases, it is not hard to understand why they emerged.

However, when we see those types of METROPOLITAN buildings in urban settings with normal condition, as opposed to extremely dense condition, we cannot easily guess why they are there. As a matter of fact, that is what happens in Boston. What do we have to expect when we see an air right of Boston Medical over Massachusetts Avenue in South Boston where there are plenty of lands around. What would have been the reason to have office spaces on top of Government Parking Garage while there are enough office spaces and fewer parking spaces around. No matter what actual reasons influenced the city to have those types of buildings, the fact, which is more important, is that those hybrid buildings exist in Boston. Some are hybrid merge between infrastructures and buildings, some are of the hybrid building types that accommodate different uses, and some are simply hybrid above all. And most of hybrid precedents in Boston happen to emerge almost naturally not through odd implementation by "stararchitects" who tend to investigate hybrid projects in the city. And thus, even though we cannot actually understand why Cambridge happen to have a county jail in one of the highest buildings in the city, we can start reading the city through the existence of those hybrid buildings, see what demands are there in the city, and expect what types of hybrid projects the city can introduce.

In short, although Boston is not and probably would never be conceived as a METROPOLIS, it actually has lots of aspects synonymous to those of the MET-ROPOLITAN. Of course, those METROPOLITAN features are neither as big nor as many as other METROPOLISES, but at least they share major properties of being METROPOLITAN. And no matter what the present condition of Boston is, having these METROPOLITAN-like features in the city, is the result of the effort of the city to become a METROPOLIS or not, or whether it even emerges by efforts of the city or not, this is what Boston has as of now, and from understanding the current situation of Boston, we can discuss about the future of the city. Having METROPOLITAN features in this small city is a very unique character of the city, which means that this might have been the way that Boston followed, whether it was on purpose, and perhaps the way that the city should envision itself through for the future. This does not mean that the city will move towards being a METROPOLIS, but means that the city can find its own way of enhancing the identity of the city and strengthen a sustainable strategy for the city.

The research "I Want to be METROPOLITAN" is an effort to understand METROPOLITAN aspects in MINI Metropolis, especially through built environment in various scales, with a case study of Boston, so that we can understand the potential of a city and picture a growth pattern of the city based on MINI Metropolitanism. In this book, we focus on METROPOLITAN aspects of Boston that seem like to be efforts of the city to become a METROPOLIS, just as a kid saying "I want to be a doctor, when I grow up." Perhaps, it is not so much more important whether the kid actually become a doctor at the end than seeing strengths, personalities and poten-tials of the kid. Being said, the research is not to insist a MINI Metropolis, in this case Boston, has to become a METROPOLIS or even MEGA-Metropolis, but to generate various conversations and find a unique growth path for it.

Although Boston is not conceived as a metropolis, we can easily find massive efforts for developing the city as such. Through an analysis of urban/architectural case studies around the city, we can better understand where the city of Boston stands in the present economic condition, and see its potential for the near future development. The city already presents a vast capacity in its infrastructure, and networks for growth, which has not been capitalized fully. By understanding the actual capacity that the city can offer, we can implement new innovative developments that address a metropolitan way of life.

BOSTON INFRA-STRUCTURE

01

BOSTON BACKGROUND

BY: RAFAEL LUNA

Since its founding in 1630, Boston has thrived as "the little engine" that actually can, proving successful at reinvention and ingenuity. Harvard economist, Edward Glaeser, attributes much of the city's success of reinvention to its human capital. The city has been able to take advantage of a multitude of situations in order to grow. When it could no longer export to England during its colonial period, it started exporting to the South, creating a triangle trade between the West Indies, England and Boston until, eventually, New York and Philadelphia took over the route. In order to gain an edge again, Boston started trading farther, investing development of sea travel and ships, bringing in great wealth for the city and expanding the shipping industry. When steam ships gained the market share over Boston sailboats, Boston moved to manufacturing. When manufacturing moved out of the city, Bostonians yet again thought of new industries to capitalize on, such as engineering, computers, finances, consulting, and bio technologies. Edward Glaeser explains this transition between industries in his book, "Triumph of the City," where Boston is categorized not only as a successful city, but as "the smart city." The nature of Boston as a smart city can be attributed to it's relation to its abundant educational institutions, and the culture of prioritizing education since the 1630's. It established the first public school, first college, first public library. It now houses 35 universities within the boundaries of administrative Boston, and over 100 colleges and universities in the Greater Boston Area. This has maintained a steady economy in the city. Almost a third of the population of administrative Boston either studies at, or is employed by, one of these institutions. The education industry alone generates over $4.9 billion a year of the city's Gross Domestic Product.

What is Boston's Metropolitan condition? Is it just a big college town? It's not wrong to categorize it as such since its top ranking schools have been a magnet of talent and innovation to the city. The city of Boston has been ranked 1st in the world as an innovation city, and we have the culture of being a city of firsts. Ed Glaeser suggests that this relationship of attracting smart people into the city, has been a key to the success. Again, this is an economical success, but where does it stand as an urban setting. For the purposes of this study, we are more interested in the growth of the city as an urban physical setting analyzing its built environment rather than it's social, or economical condition.

In the 1820's, Boston had a land area of 12 sq-km. As waves of immigrants started to arrive, Boston faced the challenge of housing a rapidly increasing population. In a matter of one hundred years, Boston increased it's land area to 125 sq-km, the area we know today. It reached it's population peak in the 1950's at around 800,000, and in a matter of 30 years lost a quarter of its population. Since the 1980's the population of Boston has remained around 600,000. This raises questions about the city's urban fabric; for example, what happened to the building stock that housed that extra 200,000 people? Or why was there not more vertical construction in the city early in the 20th century when the population growth was soaring? In the first half of the 20th century only two high-rise buildings were erected: the Custom House in 1915, and the Berkeley Building in 1947. Instead of building vertically, Boston adopted a strategy of low-rise density growth. Boston's density is, perhaps surprisingly, the same as London's, and London also lacks the extreme skyline of a city like New York. The majority of London's urban fabric is built by the Georgian Terrace, much like row-houses, and brownstones in Boston. Yet, we are hesitant to compare Boston to London in the context of the Metropolitan city. Similarly, Boston's land area is comparable to the land area of Paris; in fact, the land area of Paris is a bit smaller at 105 sqkm. Paris is also not a skyscraper driven city, but the Haussmannian urban fabric dominates the entire 105 sq-km in a layer of total urbanity. One does not think of Paris as an incomplete city. Boston on the other hand, with it's 125 sq-km is perceived to be much smaller, closer to its original size of 12sqkm. The perceived area of Boston has been focused around neighborhoods central to tourists, and around campus neighborhoods for students. This is only about 5% of the total area of Boston, and there is a general sentiment that this is Boston. This generates a cap on the development of Boston, which can be a weakness as much as a strength.

Focusing on that centralized area of Boston has enabled Boston to market itself as a boutique city. When PRAUD met with Kairos Shen, chief City Planner at the Boston Redevelopment Authority, he discussed the notion of Boston's desire to be Cosmopolitan, as opposed to Metropolitan. Boston has a very strong marketability because it has retained its boutique characteristic. The scale of the city is very manageable and nonthreatening for new-comers. It is a city that will never grow to

SINCE THE 1980'S THE POPULATION OF BOSTON HAS REMAINED AROUND 600,000

"

THE SCALE OF THE CITY IS VERY MANAGEABLE AND NONTHREATENING FOR NEW-COMERS. IT IS A CITY THAT WILL NEVER GROW TO BE ANOTHER NEW YORK

"

be another New York. As a boutique city, Boston is more comparable to Washington DC, Seattle, and San Francisco in scale, density, and culture. Comparing Boston to New York is not very productive. The charm of being boutique attracts around 19 to 20 million visitors to Boston a year. Quincy market is one of the most visited places in the United States of America. A city of 600,000 has to manage 20 million.

On the other hand, the myopic focus on the development of only the central neighborhoods of the city is evident in many of the new proposals for large construction projects. Since 2010 there have been 12 proposals for high-rise buildings, 6 of which are as tall as the Prudential or taller. Not all of them have been approved, but the idea of such proposals is debatable for a city that hasn't increased in population in over 60 years. The population in Boston hasn't increased, but it has changed in demographics. One in three people in Boston are between the ages of 20 to 34. Boston is not only one of oldest built cities, but it's also the youngest city in terms of its population, creating a unique dynamism. So, new construction in a sense should focus on addressing the 5% central Boston, and a young population within an old city fabric. Restricted by limited available land, historic building regulations, and increasing real estate prices, we can assume that a cultured city like Boston would develop particular hybrid buildings and urban studies to address such issues.

Boston, as an innovative city, also presents the potential for being a lab for urban experimentation. In the 1960's, the Japanese architect and urbanist, Kenzo Tange, was invited to teach an advance urban design studio at MIT called "25,000 People Over Boston." During this period he developed the concept for what would become his famous "Tokyo Bay" project. More recently at Harvard, Rem Koolhaas developed a masterplan for the Allston campus that called for a rerouting of the Charles river. At first glance it would seem ludicrous to reroute such an iconic river, but thinking about that nature of land reclamation of Boston (the Charles river was mostly man formed), shaping it again to unify the Harvard Campus is not that far fetched.

For these previously mentioned historical anecdotes, Boston presents the perfect conditions for this study. We will be analyzing further its growth and composition, its development of urban cores, its architectural interventions, and furthermore its potential for the future.

CHRONOLOGY

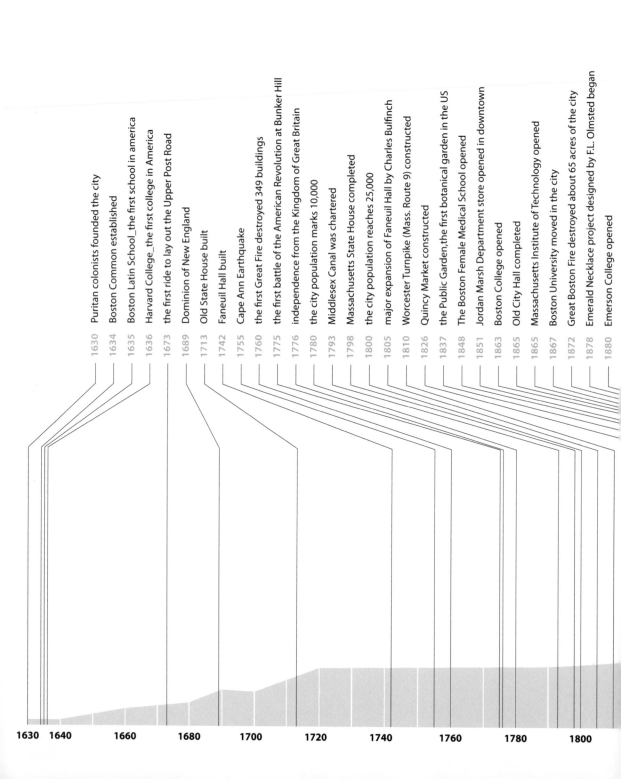

1630	Puritan colonists founded the city
1634	Boston Common established
1635	Boston Latin School_the first school in america
1636	Harvard College_the first college in America
1673	the first ride to lay out the Upper Post Road
1689	Dominion of New England
1713	Old State House built
1742	Faneuil Hall built
1755	Cape Ann Earthquake
1760	the first Great Fire destroyed 349 buildings
1775	the first battle of the American Revolution at Bunker Hill
1776	independence from the Kingdom of Great Britain
1780	the city population marks 10,000
1793	Middlesex Canal was chartered
1798	Massachusetts State House completed
1800	the city population reaches 25,000
1805	major expansion of Faneuil Hall by Charles Bulfinch
1810	Worcester Turnpike (Mass. Route 9) constructed
1826	Quincy Market constructed
1837	the Public Garden, the first botanical garden in the US
1848	The Boston Female Medical School opened
1851	Jordan Marsh Department store opened in downtown
1863	Boston College opened
1865	Old City Hall completed
1865	Massachusetts Institute of Technology opened
1867	Boston University moved in the city
1872	Great Boston Fire destroyed about 65 acres of the city
1878	Emerald Necklace project designed by F.L. Olmsted began
1880	Emerson College opened

1630 1640   1660   1680   1700   1720   1740   1760   1780   1800

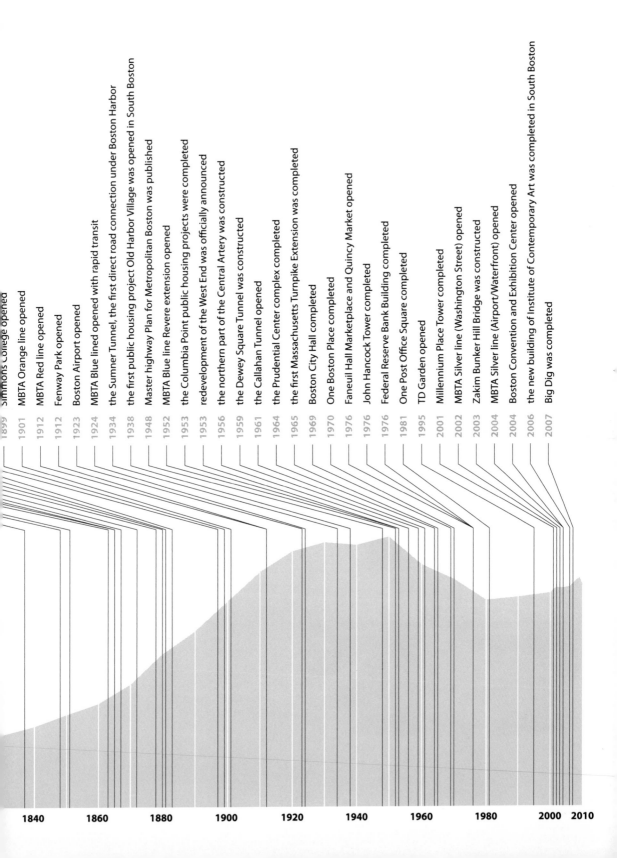

Simmons College opened — 1899
MBTA Orange line opened — 1901
MBTA Red line opened — 1912
Fenway Park opened — 1912
Boston Airport opened — 1923
MBTA Blue lined opened with rapid transit — 1924
the Sumner Tunnel, the first direct road connection under Boston Harbor — 1934
the first public housing project Old Harbor Village was opened in South Boston — 1938
Master highway Plan for Metropolitan Boston was published — 1948
MBTA Blue line Revere extension opened — 1952
the Columbia Point public housing projects were completed — 1953
redevelopment of the West End was officially announced — 1953
the northern part of the Central Artery was constructed — 1956
the Dewey Square Tunnel was constructed — 1959
the Callahan Tunnel opened — 1961
the Prudential Center complex completed — 1964
the first Massachusetts Turnpike Extension was completed — 1965
Boston City Hall completed — 1969
One Boston Place completed — 1970
Faneuil Hall Marketplace and Quincy Market opened — 1976
John Hancock Tower completed — 1976
Federal Reserve Bank Building completed — 1976
One Post Office Square completed — 1981
TD Garden opened — 1995
Millennium Place Tower completed — 2001
MBTA Silver line (Washington Street) opened — 2002
Zakim Bunker Hill Bridge was constructed — 2003
MBTA Silver line (Airport/Waterfront) opened — 2004
Boston Convention and Exhibition Center opened — 2004
the new building of Institute of Contemporary Art was completed in South Boston — 2006
Big Dig was completed — 2007

1840   1860   1880   1900   1920   1940   1960   1980   2000   2010

LANDFILL TRANSFORMATION

1. WEST COVE
1803-1863

2. MILL POND
1807-1829

3. SOUTH COVE
1806-1843

4. EAST COVE
1823-1874

5. SOUTH BOSTON
1836-NOW

6. SOUTH BAY
1850-NOW

7. BACK BAY
1857-1894

8. CHARLESTOWN AND MIT

9. FENWAY
1878-1890

10. EAST BOSTON
1880-NOW

11. EAST BOSTON
1883-1900

12. COLUMBUS PARK
1890-1901

13. LOGAN AIRPORT
1922-NOW

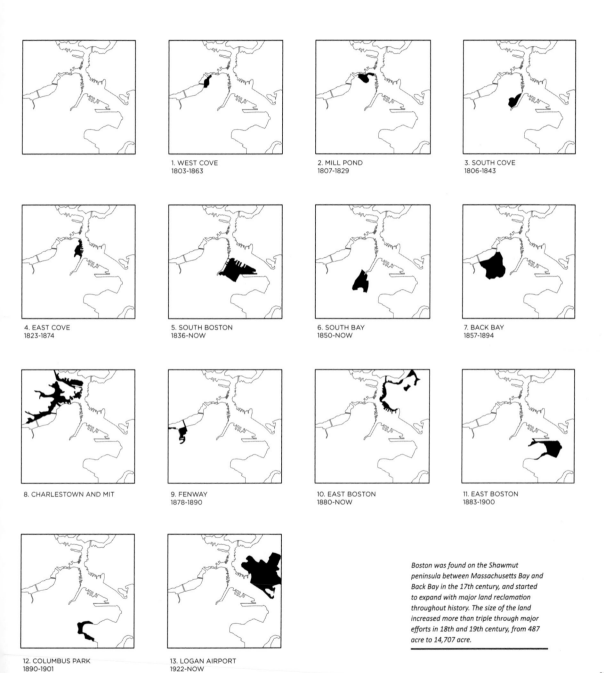

1. WEST COVE
1803-1863

2. MILL POND
1807-1829

3. SOUTH COVE
1806-1843

4. EAST COVE
1823-1874

5. SOUTH BOSTON
1836-NOW

6. SOUTH BAY
1850-NOW

7. BACK BAY
1857-1894

8. CHARLESTOWN AND MIT

9. FENWAY
1878-1890

10. EAST BOSTON
1880-NOW

11. EAST BOSTON
1883-1900

12. COLUMBUS PARK
1890-1901

13. LOGAN AIRPORT
1922-NOW

Boston was found on the Shawmut peninsula between Massachusetts Bay and Back Bay in the 17th century, and started to expand with major land reclamation throughout history. The size of the land increased more than triple through major efforts in 18th and 19th century, from 487 acre to 14,707 acre.

LANDFILL TRANSFORMATION

West Cove

Mill Pond

South Cove

East Cove

South Boston

487 ACRE

1,363

1630 1640 1660 1680 1700 1720 1740 1760 1780 1800

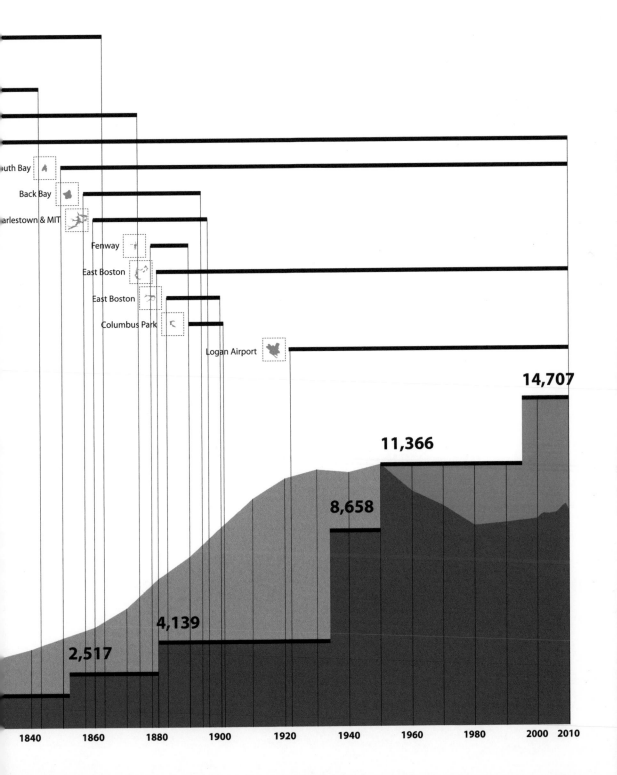

uth Bay
Back Bay
arlestown & MIT
Fenway
East Boston
East Boston
Columbus Park
Logan Airport

2,517
4,139
8,658
11,366
14,707

1840   1860   1880   1900   1920   1940   1960   1980   2000 2010

METROPOLITAN BOSTON

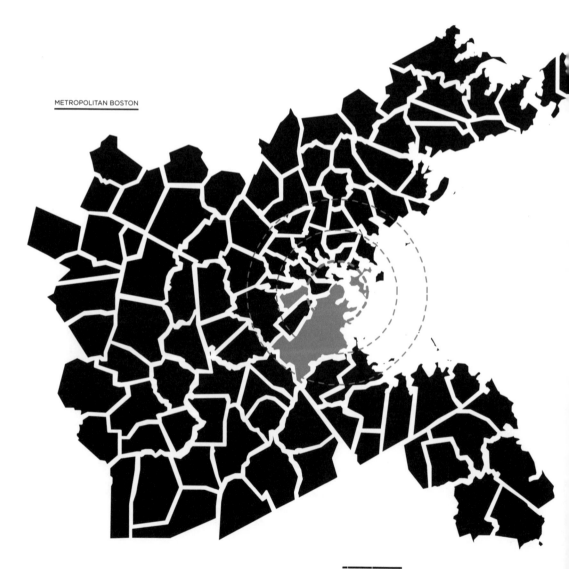

0   10 Km

I WANT TO BE METROPOLITAN

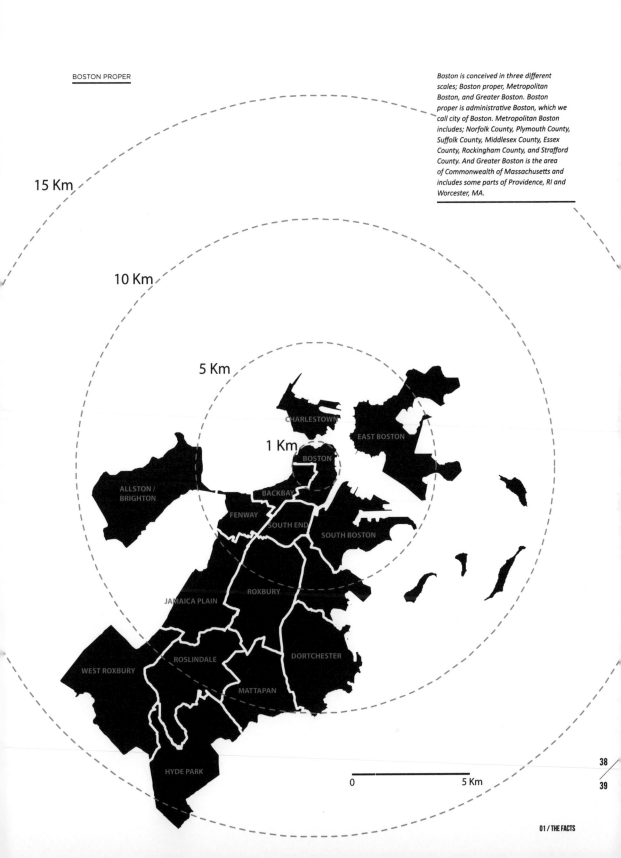

Boston is conceived in three different scales; Boston proper, Metropolitan Boston, and Greater Boston. Boston proper is administrative Boston, which we call city of Boston. Metropolitan Boston includes; Norfolk County, Plymouth County, Suffolk County, Middlesex County, Essex County, Rockingham County, and Strafford County. And Greater Boston is the area of Commonwealth of Massachusetts and includes some parts of Providence, RI and Worcester, MA.

15 Km

10 Km

5 Km

1 Km

CHARLESTOWN

EAST BOSTON

BOSTON

ALLSTON / BRIGHTON

BACKBAY

FENWAY

SOUTH END

SOUTH BOSTON

JAMAICA PLAIN

ROXBURY

ROSLINDALE

DORTCHESTER

WEST ROXBURY

MATTAPAN

HYDE PARK

0   5 Km

801,444

Max Population in 1950

Current Population

617,594

same level as 1905

562,994
same level as 1900

The population of Boston reached maximum in the 1950s and lost more than 240,000 people in thirty years. Ever since, it took another thirty years to recover 50,000 people, which is still 190,000 people less than the population in the 1950s. It implies the fact that Boston actually can handle 200,000 more residents than now with infrastructures back then.

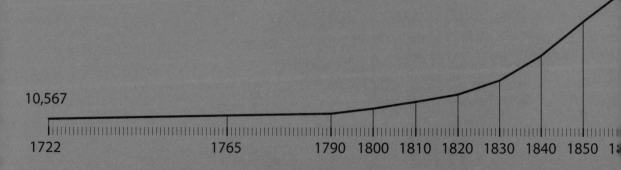

10,567

| 1722 | 1765 | 1790 | 1800 | 1810 | 1820 | 1830 | 1840 | 1850 | 18 |

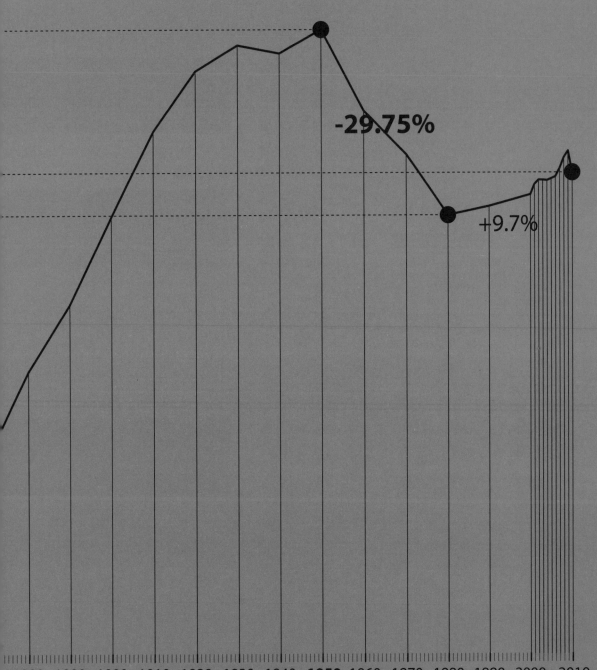

-29.75%

+9.7%

1880 1890 1900 1910 1920 1930 1940 **1950** 1960 1970 1980 1990 2000 2010

Year	Population	Change
1722	10,567	—
1765	**15,520**	**+46.9%**
1790	18,320	+18.0%
1800	24,937	+36.1%
1810	33,787	+35.5%
1820	43,298	+28.1%
1830	**61,392**	**+41.8%**
1840	**93,383**	**+52.1%**
1850	**136,881**	**+46.6%**
1860	177,840	+29.9%
1870	**250,526**	**+40.9%**
1880	**362,839**	**+44.8%**
1890	448,477	+23.6%
1900	560,892	+25.1%
1910	670,585	+19.6%
1920	748,060	+11.6%
1930	781,188	+4.4%
1940	770,816	−1.3%
1950	801,444	+4.0%
1960	**697,197**	**−13.0%**
1970	**641,071**	**−8.1%**
1980	**562,994**	**−12.2%**
1990	574,283	+2.0%
2000	589,141	+2.6%
2001	602,380	+2.2%
2002	607,931	+0.9%
2003	607,871	−0.0%
2004	607,367	−0.1%
2005	609,690	+0.4%
2006	612,192	+0.4%
2007	622,748	+1.7%
2008	636,748	+2.2%
2009	645,169	+1.3%
2010	617,594	−4.3%

First wave of immigrants
35,000 Irish

Irish, Germans, Italians, Lebanese, Syrians, French Canadians, Russian Jews and Polish Jews

Industry moved out of the city as the factories became obsolete.

DEMOGRAPHICS

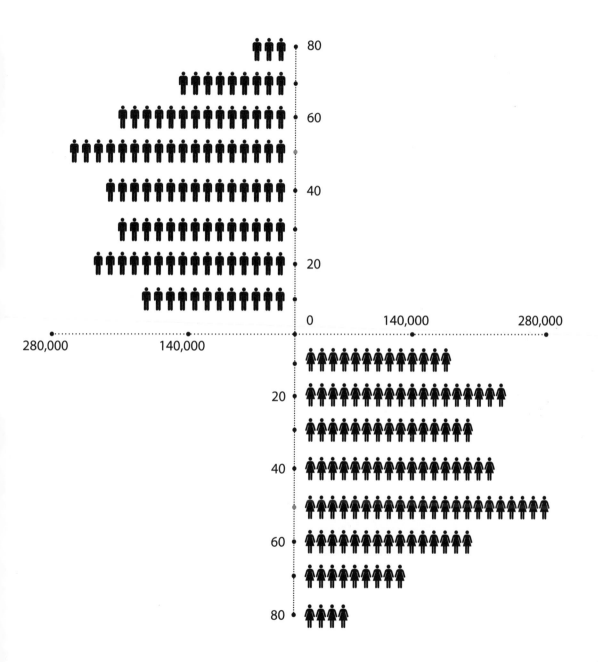

RESIDENTS PER ACRE OF RESIDENTIAL LAND

Population Concentration (metro Boston)
Residents per acre of residential land

- ● Greater than 20
- ● 15-20
- ● 10-15
- ● 5-10
- • Less than 5

In the 1950's the population of Boston peaked at around 800,000. In the following decades it dropped to 560,000 and stabilized at around 600,000. So where did all those people go? By looking at the density map of the metropolitan area of Boston, we can understand that the neighboring cities and suburbs support that extra population. Cities like Malden, Everett, Somerville, have a high density rate at a close proximity of administrative Boston. Their proximity allows for quick commuting in and out of Boston, and although these are independent cities, they work as a single area defined as Metro-Boston.

BEDFORD

BURLINGTON

WAKEFIELD

PEABODY

SALEM

WOBURN STONEHAM

SAUGUS

LEXINGTON

WINCHESTER

MELROSE

LYNN

MALDEN

ARLINGTON

MEDFORD

EVERETT REVERE

SOMERVILLE

CHELSEA

WALTHAM

WATERTOWN

CAMBRIDGE

WESTON

BOSTON

NEWTON

BROOKLINE

WELLESLEY

NEEDHAM

MILTON

QUINCY

DEDHAM

BRAINTREE

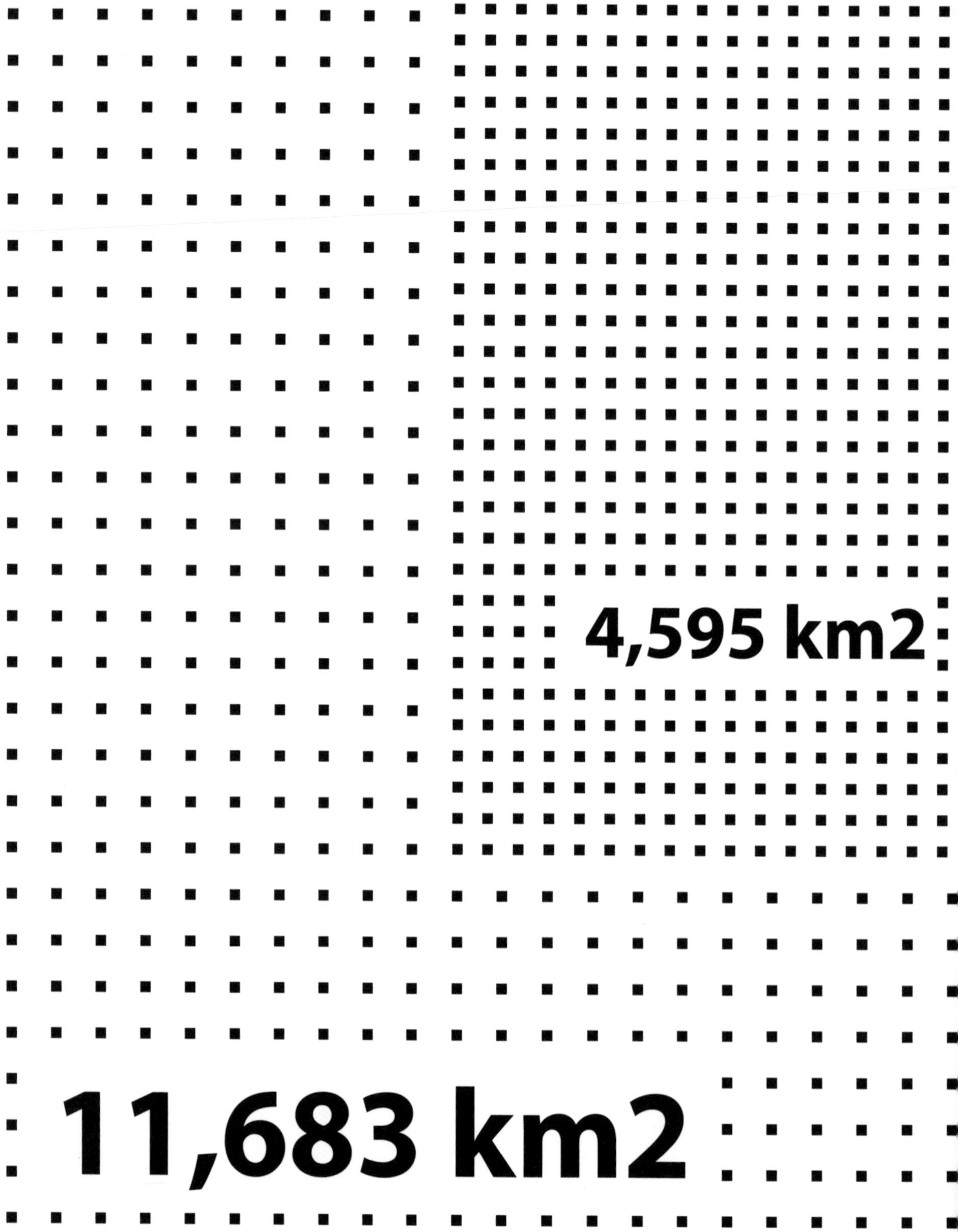

4,595 km2

11,683 km2

I WANT TO BE METROPOLITAN

125 km2

617,594
City Population

City Center Density 4,924 people / km2

4,032,484
Urban Population

4,522,858
Metro Population

THE METROPOLIS

BY: RAFAEL LUNA

In his 1978 manifesto, Delirious New York, Rem Koolhaas defines the metropolis as a condition of explosive technological growth coupled with a massive increase in population in a limited space. This condition is exemplified by the turn of the 20th century, when rapid industrialization produced an influx of migration into the cities as people sought to fill nascent job opportunities. The merging population created new social dynamics, and with them new possibilities in architecture that would ultimately become the birth of metropolitan architecture. In order to understand the current metropolitan condition, it is necessary to reflect on the transition that occurred during the turn of the 20th century and the effects that it had on both work and life in the city.

Karl Marx described the resulting social condition as a stratification of social classes: the ruling class (bourgeoisie) and the working class (proletariat). Stratification of social classes belied a socioeconomic imbalance, where property and power were concentrated in the hands of the few. This imbalance, coupled with a surging population of workers supporting growing industries, meant that the housing for the proletariat in the city quickly became inadequate.

Cities were spreading as an industrial fields. It could be conceived that the Metropolis and the urban setting would just turn into vast districts of fabrication and production. This implies that architecture would cease to be; the urban setting would simply become industry. This was expanded by the Czech artist and architecture critic, Karel Teige, who reflected on the social conditions of the proletariat, their life of reproduction, and their lack of housing. He suggested that an "International Modern Architecture" should tackle the problems of the minimum dwelling to solve the social implications of collective housing. Spaces would no longer be classified as the traditional bedroom, kitchen, living room, but rather would reflect the living and working conditions of the time. A space might consist of areas for sleeping, eating, and resting without implying a classification or assigned program.

Advances in technology also facilitated the invention of new architectural spaces with the possibility of new social interaction and higher density. The invention of the safety-catch on elevators by Otis paved the way for the modern skyscraper. This allowed for singular spaces, non-specific to the building, at different levels. This generated a new layering effect where it was up to the human imagination to device endless possibilities of programming to occur within a single building. It also implied that housing could be minimized since these metropolitan buildings would

48
49

provide all the amenities and stimulation that were before desired from a single dwelling.

German sociologist, Georg Simmel, described the social implications of rapid industry and minimum dwelling as a problem of individuality. There is a jump in scale from the slow moving rural condition to the rapidly moving, explosive Metropolis. The individual becomes detached and pursues individuality as a mode of existing in the metropolis. The rapid pace generates two things: first, the detached individual that shies from interaction, and second, a constant stimulation of the senses, which lead to a "Blasé attitude."

Simmel:

"The blasé attitude results first from the rapidly changing and closely compressed contrasting stimulation of the nerves. From this, the enhancement of metropolitan intellectuality, also, seems originally to stem. Therefore, stupid people who are not intellectually alive in the first place usually are not exactly blasé. A life in boundless pursuit of pleasure makes one blasé because it agitates the nerves to their strongest reactivity for such a long time that they finally cease to react at all. In the same way, through the rapidity and contradictoriness of their changes, more harmless impressions force such violent responses, tearing the nerves so brutally hither and thither that their last reserves of strength are spent; and if one remains in the same milieu they have no time to gather new strength. An incapacity thus emerges to react to new sensations with the appropriate energy. This constitutes that blasé attitude which, in fact, every metropolitan child shows when compared with children of quieter and less changeable milieus."

So, where is the Metropolis moving towards as we rapidly advance in technology, and urbanity continues its domination? Areas like BosWash, Benelux, and Blue Banana exist where strips of constant construction make it difficult to identify where the Metropolis ends and the "Megalopolis" begins. What is urban and what is suburban? Our built environment is rapidly responding to these conditions by means of new typologies that reflect a new way of life.

Looking back, it is easy to understand the concept of the metropolis in the context of the early 20th century with the industrial revolution pushing the growth of

ADVANCES IN TECHNOLOGY ALSO FACILITATED THE INVENTION OF NEW ARCHITECTURAL SPACES WITH THE POSSIBILITY OF NEW SOCIAL INTERACTION AND HIGHER DENSITY.

"

the city, generating jobs, increasing migration into a limited area. These conditions used to define the metropolis. People would move from the country to the city. Now we have people moving and operating between cities. What defines the metropolis today? Half the world's population lives in urban settings. Still we cannot simply analogize cities like Boston to New York, Zurich to London, or Melbourne to Tokyo. Under the 20th century definition, all of these cities are metropolises, but in the 21st century, these metropolises ask to be subdivided and categorized into different levels.

Reflecting on Georg Simmel's description of the "blasé attitude," a metropolis provides constant stimulation until you reach a level of uncaring, or familiarity with what was once new and exciting. But 21st century Metropolises, can also be categorized by levels of "blasé." More simply put, how long can you live in a city before getting bored? How long do you need to visit a city in order to explore it and enjoy it? A week in Boston, a month in Barcelona, a year in Tokyo? Cities like Tokyo have a tradition of maximizing their urbanity by making use of every available parcel and hybridizing buildings to the point that they are fields of constant urbanity, which in turn produces a field of constant stimulation. This is a very particular characteristic that hints at ways to classify cities.

The point is that we can no longer rely on one classification of Metropolis, the scale of some cities are not directly comparable. We cannot apply rules of fast growth that are appropriate in Shanghai to a city like Seattle, or strategies for congestion in Caracas to Boston. The term metropolis, still implies a stimulating urban setting, it has connotations of density, centers of technology, and opportunity; but when half the world is urban, the term metropolis seems useless by itself. For this reason we introduce the MINI-metropolis to classify these cities that are smaller, gradually growing, more stable, yet maintain a high level of culture and global influence; cities like Boston, Zurich, Amsterdam. It is important to understand the different levels of metropolitanism so that we can maximize the potential of each city, and rule out strategies that may not apply for future growth.

25

TOP U.S CITIES BY
POPULATION

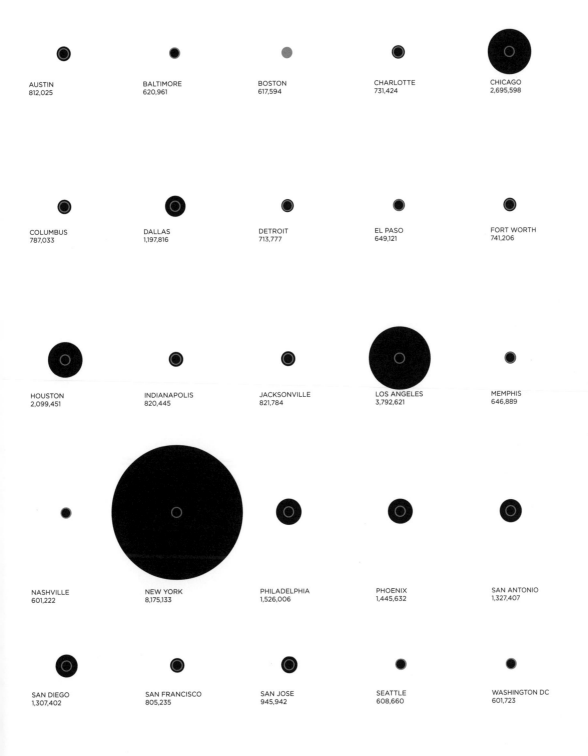

AUSTIN
812,025

BALTIMORE
620,961

BOSTON
617,594

CHARLOTTE
731,424

CHICAGO
2,695,598

COLUMBUS
787,033

DALLAS
1,197,816

DETROIT
713,777

EL PASO
649,121

FORT WORTH
741,206

HOUSTON
2,099,451

INDIANAPOLIS
820,445

JACKSONVILLE
821,784

LOS ANGELES
3,792,621

MEMPHIS
646,889

NASHVILLE
601,222

NEW YORK
8,175,133

PHILADELPHIA
1,526,006

PHOENIX
1,445,632

SAN ANTONIO
1,327,407

SAN DIEGO
1,307,402

SAN FRANCISCO
805,235

SAN JOSE
945,942

SEATTLE
608,660

WASHINGTON DC
601,723

TOP U.S CITIES BY
AREA

AUSTIN
772

BALTIMORE
210

BOSTON
125

CHARLOTTE
771

CHICAGO
589

COLUMBUS
563

DALLAS
882

DETROIT
360

EL PASO
661

FORT WORTH
880

HOUSTON
1,553

INDIANAPOLIS
936

JACKSONVILLE
1,935

LOS ANGELES
1,214

MEMPHIS
816

NASHVILLE
1,231

NEW YORK
784

PHILADELPHIA
347

PHOENIX
1,338

SAN ANTONIO
1,194

SAN DIEGO
842

SAN FRANCISCO
121

SAN JOSE
457

SEATTLE
217

WASHINGTON DC
158

TOP U.S CITIES BY
DENSITY

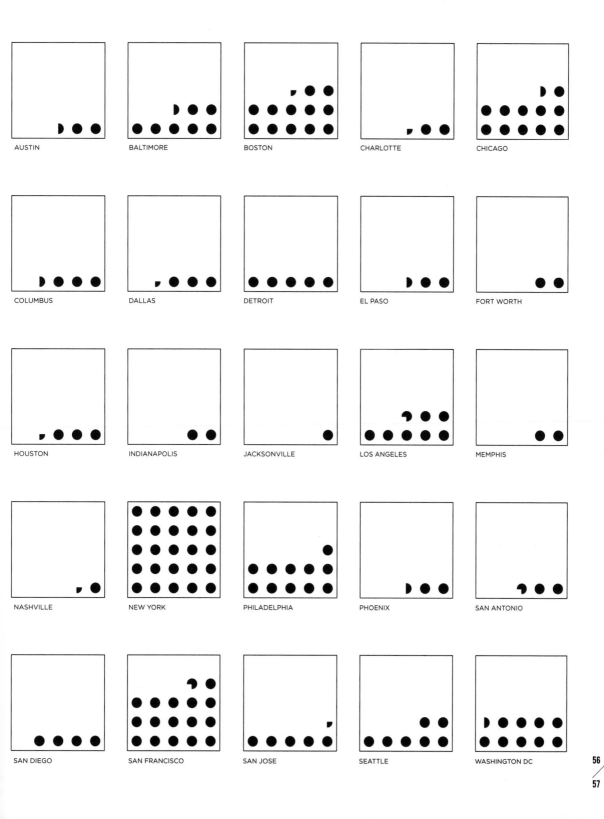

AUSTIN

BALTIMORE

BOSTON

CHARLOTTE

CHICAGO

COLUMBUS

DALLAS

DETROIT

EL PASO

FORT WORTH

HOUSTON

INDIANAPOLIS

JACKSONVILLE

LOS ANGELES

MEMPHIS

NASHVILLE

NEW YORK

PHILADELPHIA

PHOENIX

SAN ANTONIO

SAN DIEGO

SAN FRANCISCO

SAN JOSE

SEATTLE

WASHINGTON DC

JACKSONVILLE	NEW YORK	NEW YORK	
HOUSTON	LOS ANGELES	SAN FRANCISCO	
PHOENIX	CHICAGO	BOSTON	
NASHVILLE	HOUSTON	CHICAGO	
LOS ANGELES	PHILADELPHIA	PHILADELPHIA	
SAN ANTONIO	PHOENIX	WASHINGTON DC	
INDIANAPOLIS	SAN ANTONIO	LOS ANGELES	
DALLAS	SAN DIEGO	BALTIMORE	
FORT WORTH	DALLAS	SEATTLE	
SAN DIEGO	SAN JOSE	SAN JOSE	
MEMPHIS	JACKSONVILLE	DETROIT	
NEW YORK	INDIANAPOLIS	SAN DIEGO	
AUSTIN	AUSTIN	COLUMBUS	
CHARLOTTE	SAN FRANCISCO	DALLAS	
EL PASO	COLUMBUS	HOUSTON	
CHICAGO	FORT WORTH	SAN ANTONIO	
COLUMBUS	CHARLOTTE	PHOENIX	
SAN JOSE	DETROIT	AUSTIN	
DETROIT	EL PASO	EL PASO	
PHILADELPHIA	MEMPHIS	CHARLOTTE	
SEATTLE	BALTIMORE	INDIANAPOLIS	
BALTIMORE	BOSTON	FORT WORTH	
WASHINGTON DC	SEATTLE	MEMPHIS	
BOSTON	WASHINGTON DC	NASHVILLE	
SAN FRANCISCO	NASHVILLE	JACKSONVILLE	

MOST
COMPARABLE
US CITIES

There is an unspoken rivalry between Boston and New York, that could easily be explained as a Red-Sox vs Yankees rivalry. When population, density, and area are compared, we can find that Boston is far from being a comparable city to New York. Boston is more comparable to cities like San Francisco, Seattle, Washington DC. These are also cities that we can define as Mini-metropolises. These cities are not going to be the next New York, but that is not their goal either. These cities succeed from their unique characters, comparable to a boutique hotels. As such, there should be some framework of understanding and operation for these comparable cities.

AREA

POPULATION

DENSITY

Washington DC
158 Km2

Baltimore
620,961

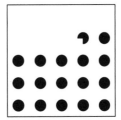

San Francisco
6,700 People/Km2

Boston
125 Km2

Boston
617,594

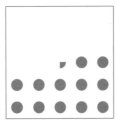

Boston
4,900 People/Km2

San Francisco
121 Km2

Seattle
608,660

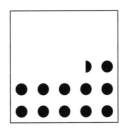

Chicago
4,600 People/Km2

INTERNATIONAL CITIES

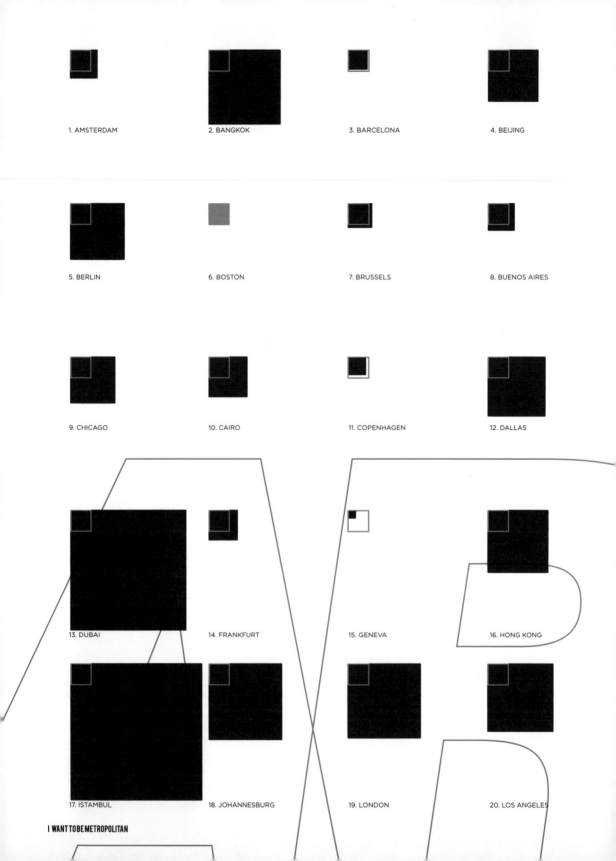

1. AMSTERDAM

2. BANGKOK

3. BARCELONA

4. BEIJING

5. BERLIN

6. BOSTON

7. BRUSSELS

8. BUENOS AIRES

9. CHICAGO

10. CAIRO

11. COPENHAGEN

12. DALLAS

13. DUBAI

14. FRANKFURT

15. GENEVA

16. HONG KONG

17. ISTAMBUL

18. JOHANNESBURG

19. LONDON

20. LOS ANGELES

I WANT TO BE METROPOLITAN

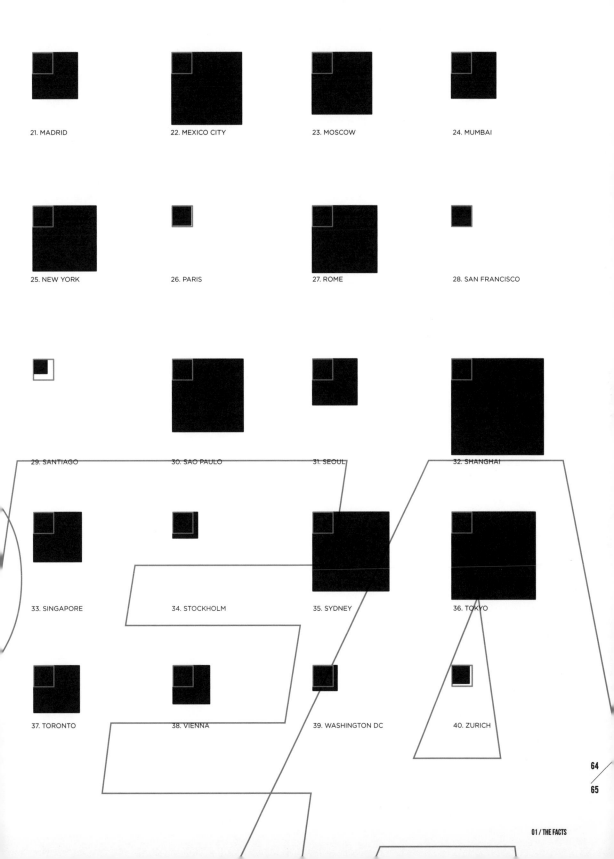

21. MADRID

22. MEXICO CITY

23. MOSCOW

24. MUMBAI

25. NEW YORK

26. PARIS

27. ROME

28. SAN FRANCISCO

29. SANTIAGO

30. SAO PAULO

31. SEOUL

32. SHANGHAI

33. SINGAPORE

34. STOCKHOLM

35. SYDNEY

36. TOKYO

37. TORONTO

38. VIENNA

39. WASHINGTON DC

40. ZURICH

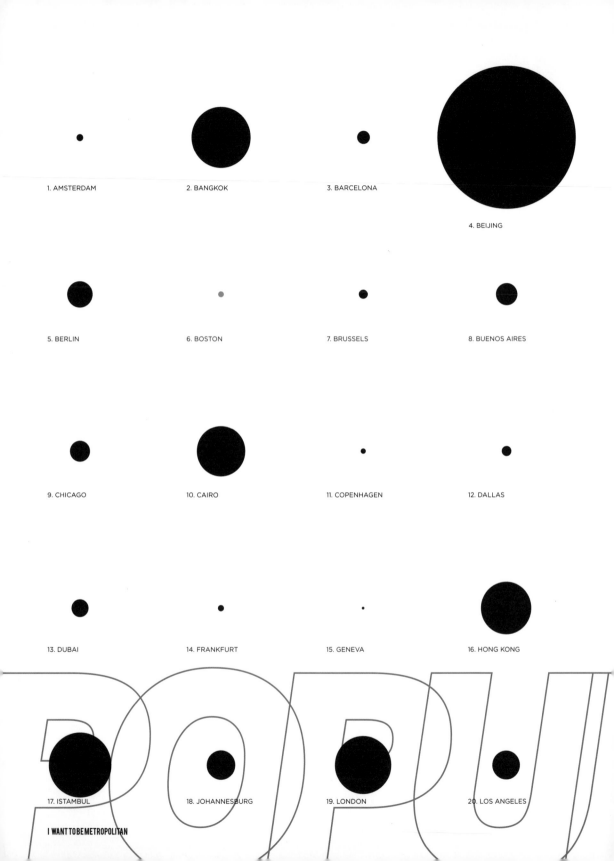

1. AMSTERDAM

2. BANGKOK

3. BARCELONA

4. BEIJING

5. BERLIN

6. BOSTON

7. BRUSSELS

8. BUENOS AIRES

9. CHICAGO

10. CAIRO

11. COPENHAGEN

12. DALLAS

13. DUBAI

14. FRANKFURT

15. GENEVA

16. HONG KONG

17. ISTAMBUL

18. JOHANNESBURG

19. LONDON

20. LOS ANGELES

I WANT TO BE METROPOLITAN

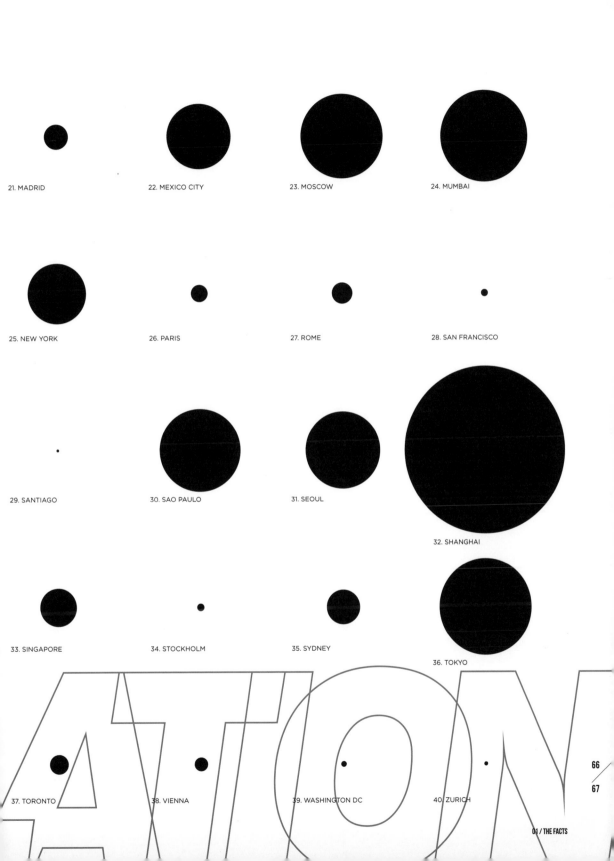

21. MADRID

22. MEXICO CITY

23. MOSCOW

24. MUMBAI

25. NEW YORK

26. PARIS

27. ROME

28. SAN FRANCISCO

29. SANTIAGO

30. SAO PAULO

31. SEOUL

32. SHANGHAI

33. SINGAPORE

34. STOCKHOLM

35. SYDNEY

36. TOKYO

37. TORONTO

38. VIENNA

39. WASHINGTON DC

40. ZURICH

01 / THE FACTS

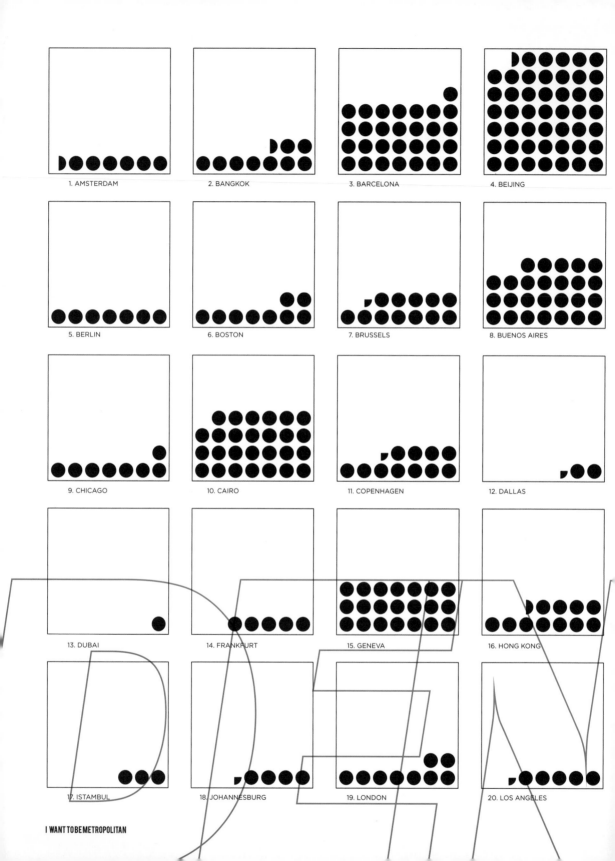

1. AMSTERDAM

2. BANGKOK

3. BARCELONA

4. BEIJING

5. BERLIN

6. BOSTON

7. BRUSSELS

8. BUENOS AIRES

9. CHICAGO

10. CAIRO

11. COPENHAGEN

12. DALLAS

13. DUBAI

14. FRANKFURT

15. GENEVA

16. HONG KONG

17. ISTAMBUL

18. JOHANNESBURG

19. LONDON

20. LOS ANGELES

I WANT TO BE METROPOLITAN

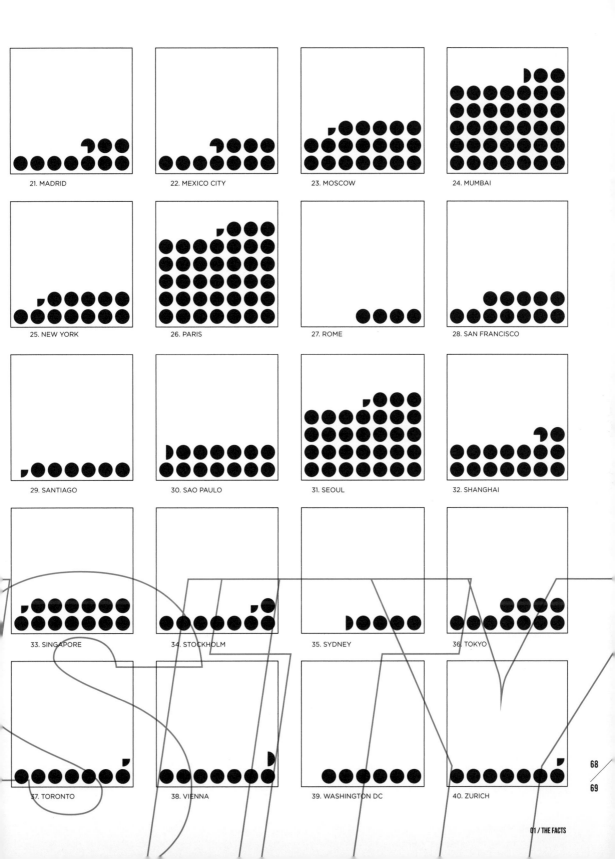

21. MADRID

22. MEXICO CITY

23. MOSCOW

24. MUMBAI

25. NEW YORK

26. PARIS

27. ROME

28. SAN FRANCISCO

29. SANTIAGO

30. SAO PAULO

31. SEOUL

32. SHANGHAI

33. SINGAPORE

34. STOCKHOLM

35. SYDNEY

36. TOKYO

37. TORONTO

38. VIENNA

39. WASHINGTON DC

40. ZURICH

MOST COMPARABLE INTERNATIONAL CITIES

....

After comparing Boston among other American cities, we find that there is a range of scale of classification and operation. But when we start comparing at a global scale, we find that Boston is quite comparable to some leading World Capitals, which leads to a discussion, of how can a city like Boston be viewed as such? The land area of Paris is actually a bit smaller than the land area of Paris, and the density of London is almost the same as Boston's. It is very difficult to conceptualize that Paris is smaller than Boston, and makes us question the perceivable area of Boston. London has been able to sustain growth while maintaining a much more comfortable scale that New York. Having a similar density, shouldn't Boston be looking at strategies implemented in London rather than compare to New York?

FRANKFURT -
679,664

PARIS -
105 KM2

LONDON -
4,978

Boston -
617,594

POPULATION

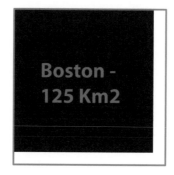

Boston -
125 Km2

AREA

Boston -
4,940

DENSITY

FRANKFURT - 10%

COPENHAGEN - 12.2%
AMSTERDAM - 26.3%
SAN FRANCISCO - 30.4%
STOCKHOLM - 37.8%
ZURICH - 39.8%
SANTIAGO - 67.5%
GENEVA - 69%

PARIS - 16%

BARCELONA - 18.4%
ZURICH - 26.4%
BRUSSELS - 28.8%
COPENHAGEN 29.6%
STOCKHOLM - 50.4%
SANTIAGO - 53.6%
BUENOS AIRES - 62.4%

LONDON - 0.8%

BANGKOK - 6.4%
STOCKHOLM - 8.4%
MADRID - 9.1%
VIENNA - 16.4%
ZURICH - 18.1%
TORONTO - 19.6%
MEXICO CITY - 20.6

IS NEW YORK A
RIVAL CITY TO BOSTON? ARE WE
TRYING BE BECOME ANOTHER
CITY LIKE NEW YORK?

?

NYC VS BOS

NKEES

SUCK!

MBTA : SUBWAY

Subway system of Boston started in 1887 with Tremont Street Subway which is the oldest subway tunnel in North America and was established three years before the New York City Subway. Once the city had elevated rail ways, but they are all removed now. Boston now has four major lines; Red, Orange, Blue and Green, and average number of riders in weekday was 628,000 in 2005.

MBTA : COMMUTER RAIL

It is a regional rail system that covers Metropolitan Boston and some part Greater Boston area. There are three major commuter rail stations in Boston; South Station, North Station and Back Bay Station. There are total twelve lines currently and the number of riders a month in average is about 10,000.

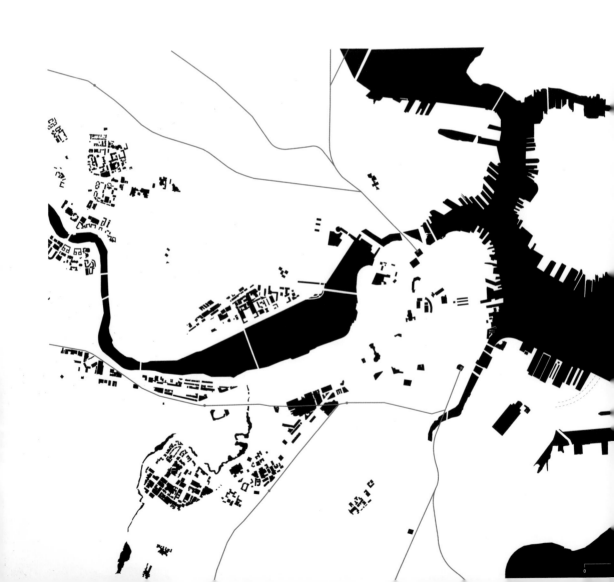

0

MBTA : BUS

The system covers Greater Boston area with more than 150 routes, and it is seventh largest system in the U.S by ridership. In 2005, there were more than 360,000 riders in weekdays in average. There are still four routes that runs as trackless trolleys which all are connecting to Red Line Harvard Station.

MBTA : COMMUTER BOAT

It is a public water transport system that covers inner harbor of Boston and regional area as well. There are total 4 routes; F1, between Boston and Hingham, F2, between downtown Boston, East Boston and Quincy, F2H, between Pemberton, downtown Boston and East Boston, and F4, between Charlestown and downtown Boston.

HUBWAY

This bike sharing program was first launched in 2011 with 60 stations and 600 bicycles around the city. It provides you an opportunity of green transit and easy connection to existing MBTA stations. It recorded more than 140,000 trips in four months since it was launched, and more stations will be installed across the Charles River in Cambridge and Somerville in 2012.

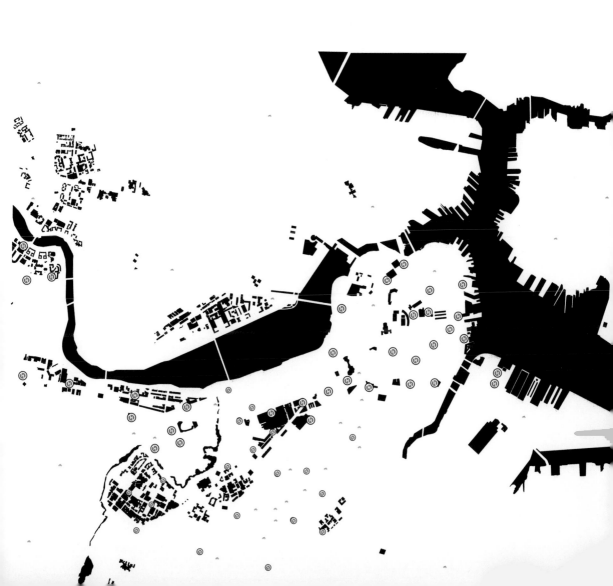

LOGAN
INTERNATIO
AIRPORT

LOGAN INTERNATIONAL AIRPORT

I-90

Airport Station

1km

ST BOSTON

Water Taxi

km

0   500 km

DIRECT FLIGHT LINES FROM BOSTON

LOGAN INTERNATIONAL AIRPORT

Logan International Airport opened in 1923, and has served as a driving force for development in the East Boston area. Logan employs around 16,000 people and in 2011 managed 28 million passengers, making it the 19th most busiest airport in the US. It is important to understand the statistics in correspondence to location. Airports in cities like Denver, Phoenix, and Detroit manage larger capacities that have no correlation to the size of the city, or actual influx into the city. Some airports serve as international hubs that are isolated from their cities, where passengers are just in traffic. Due to it's proximity to the city and accessibility, Logan International Airport has become a good marker for understanding the dynamics of Boston. During the economic recovery in the 1970's, Terminal E was the second largest international facility in the US. It has remained extremely busy for the scale of Boston, but it lost its ranking to the newer International Hub Airports, which mostly serve as transit airport to domestic destinations. Year round, Logan is ranked 19th in the US as busiest airport, but during the holidays, it is actually the 5th busiest. This is an interesting fact, since holiday travels represent more of an end destination travel. So these could represent either a lot of tourist desire to visit Boston during the Holidays, or a lot of people in Boston fly out to visit their families elsewhere. If the later is the case, it also implies that Boston is a desirable place to live.

SEA

MSP

JFK
BOS
13,561,814

SLC

EWR
LGA

SFO

DTW

BWI
PHL

DEN
25,241,962

ORD
32,171,831

IAD

LAS

CLT

LAX
28,857,755

PHX

DFW
27,100,656

ATL
43,130,585

IAH

MCO

FLL

HNL

MIA

0   500 km

25 BUSIEST AIRPORTS

SEA

BOS

SFO

LGA
EWR
JFK

DEN

ORD

LAX

MCO

0   500 km

10 BUSIEST AIRPORTS IN HOLIDAY SEASONS

BIG DIG; I-93

Big Dig is one of the biggest infrastructural projects in New England area in all time. It rerouted elevated highway I-93, that was running through in the middle of Boston, into 5.6 km long tunnel underneath. Together with the underground highway, the Ted Williams Tunnel that extends I-90 to East Boston, and Leonard P. Zakim Bunker Hill Memorial Bridge (Zakim Bridge), which is the widest, not the longest, cable-stayed bridge in the world, over the Charles River, were constructed. The construction kicked off in 1991 with Ted Williams Tunnel, most of phases were done by 2003, and finally the underground portion of the Big Dig project was completed in 2003. Rose Kennedy Greenway, which is reclaimed surface area above the tunnel, is still on the way of its development.

AIR-RIGTS; MASS. TURNPIKE

In 2000, Boston Redevelopment Authority, the Boston Transportation Department and Massachusetts Turnpike Authority released a civic vision for Turnpike Air Rights. It started with a simple perspective to repair the physical, social and economic breach caused by the railroad and the Turnpike's cut through Boston. Finally the vision was made to improve public transportation, enhance neighborhoods in the air rights, and promote the public realm by planning new pedestrian friendly connections. And air-rigt projects over the Turnpike provide the city a new opportunity to introduce a new way of development.

PRUDENTIAL DEVELOPMENT.
SEE PP. 262-265

BOSTON HYNES CONVENTION CENTER
SEE PP. 226-227

MASS. TURNPIKE

EMERALD NECKLACE

Emerald Necklace is a landscape network that almost functions as infrastructure in a way that it forms the morphology of Boston. The park system was designed in 1894 by Frederick Law Olmsted, who is also a designer of Central Park in Manhattan, to connect Boston Common, Public Garden in downtown Boston and Franklin Park in Dorchester. The Emerald Necklace runs nearly 12km through numbers of different neighborhoods in the city and it forms about 4.5 km2 park.

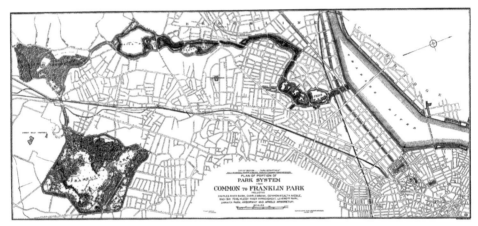

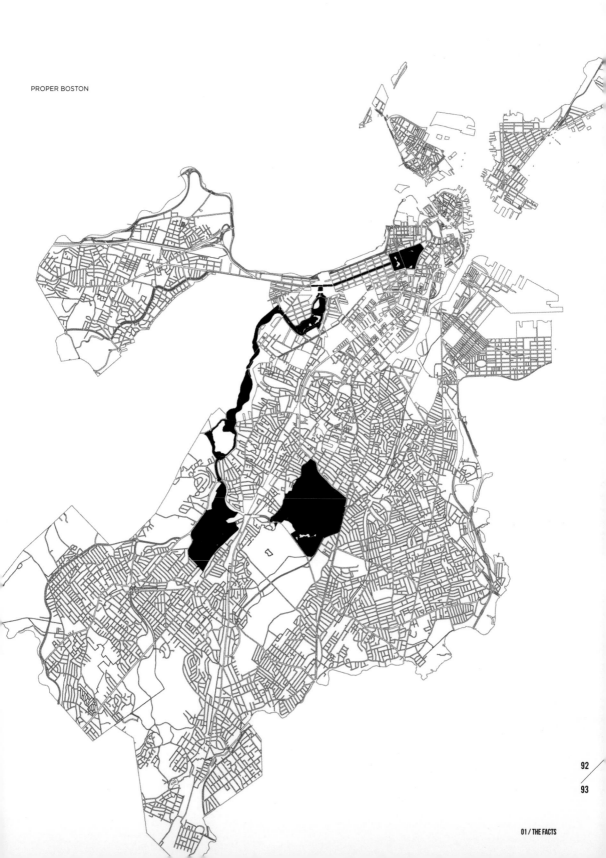

VERTICAL
BOSTON

VERTICAL BOSTON

Boston's skyline as we know it today, was mostly developed during the 1970's. From the turn of the century till the 1960's, only 2 highrises were built, the Clock tower, and the Berkeley Building. If we juxtapose the highrise building rate to the population growth rate, we notice a strange discrepancy. During the peak years in population growth, the city of Boston grew by adding land through land reclamation, but maintained a very low skyline. During the 1960's and 70's after having lost more than 200,000 residents, Boston increased it's skyscraper stock with 14 new skyscrapers, and 11 more till 2010. On the decade of 2010 to 2020 we are facing the proposal of 12 new skyscrapers, 6 being the height of the Prudential building or taller. Imagine the central area of Boston (Chinatown, Back Bay, Financial District, North End, and West End) as a single floor building, then from 1900 to 2010, Boston has built three floors. The new proposals represent building 4 more floors of Boston. The question that arises is, what should these new buildings be programed with? There is a limit to hotels and luxury condos that can be built. This present the opportunity to re-evaluate the metropolitan nature of the skyscraper and its obligations towards making the city more dynamic.

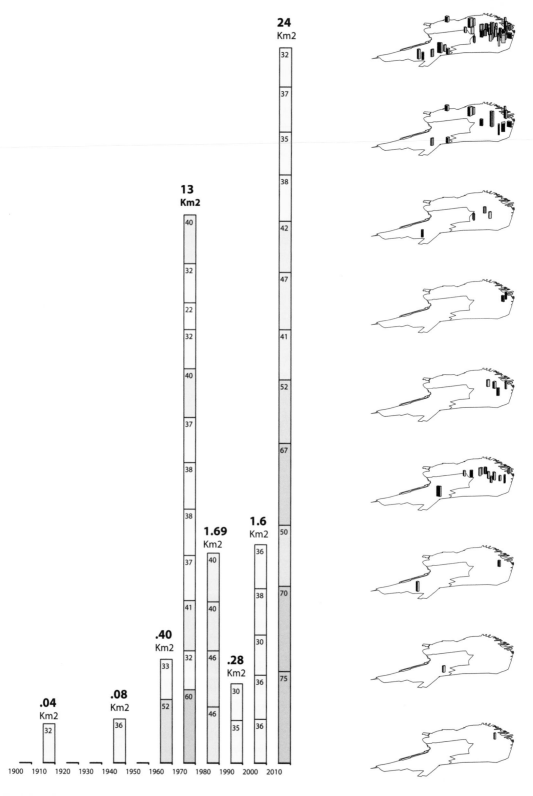

24
Km2

| 32 |
| 37 |
| 35 |
| 38 |
| 42 |
| 47 |
| 41 |
| 52 |
| 67 |
| 50 |
| 70 |
| 75 |

13
Km2

| 40 |
| 32 |
| 22 |
| 32 |
| 40 |
| 37 |
| 38 |
| 38 |
| 37 |
| 41 |
| 32 |
| 33 |
| 52 |

1.69
Km2

| 40 |
| 40 |
| 46 |
| 60 |

.40
Km2

| 33 |
| 52 |

1.6
Km2

| 36 |
| 38 |
| 30 |
| 36 |
| 36 |

.28
Km2

| 30 |
| 46 |
| 35 |

.04
Km2

| 32 |

.08
Km2

| 36 |

1900 1910 1920 1930 1940 1950 1960 1970 1980 1990 2000 2010

I WANT TO BE METROPOLITAN

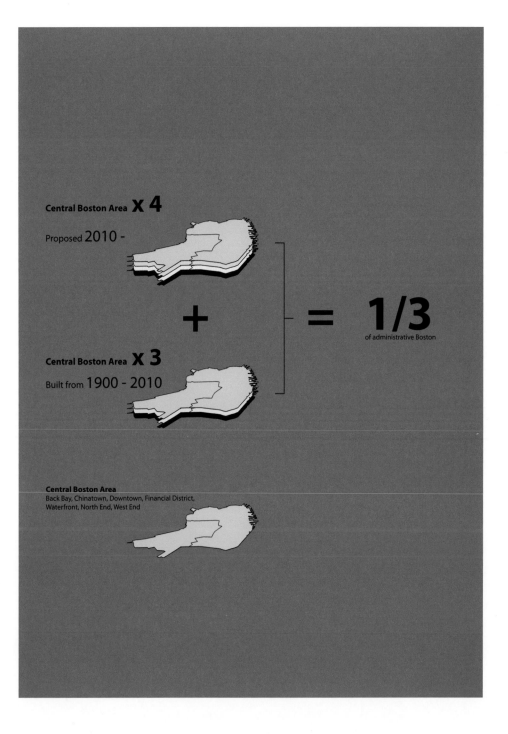

Central Boston Area **x 4**

Proposed 2010 -

+

Central Boston Area **x 3**

Built from 1900 - 2010

= **1/3**
of administrative Boston

Central Boston Area
Back Bay, Chinatown, Downtown, Financial District,
Waterfront, North End, West End

CITY PASS

PERCEIVED BOSTON

Although statistically city of Boston has similar size to inner part of Paris, mostly we think Paris is much bigger city than Boston. It is partly because what tourists perceive in Boston is less than 5% of the total area, while visitors to Paris experience most of parts of the city.

DUCK TOUR

OLD CITY TROLLEY

FREEDOM TRAIL

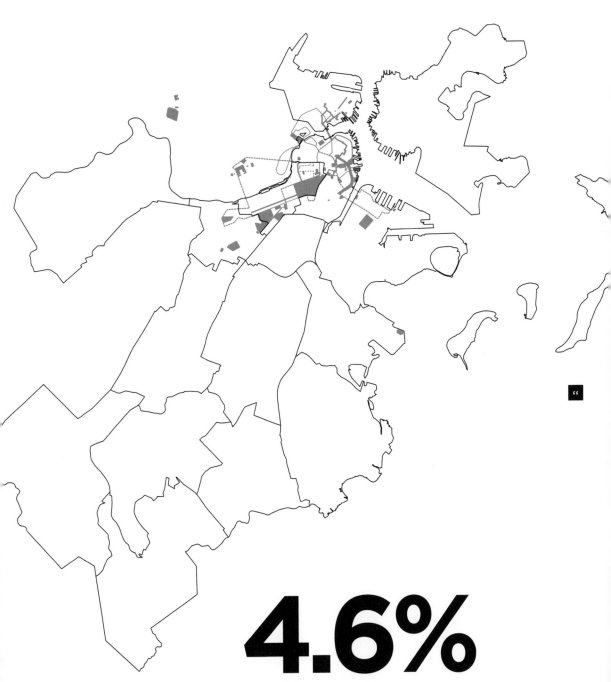

4.6%

OF THE TOTAL AREA OF BOSTON IS VISITED BY TOURISTS

WITH 20 MILLION VISITORS A YEAR, FANEUIL HALL MARKETPLACE IS 4TH THE MOST VISITED PLACE IN THE NATION AS A SINGLE DESTINATION, NEXT TO TIME SQUARE IN NEW YORK, THE LAS VEGAS STRIP, AND NATIONAL MALL IN WASHINGTON, DC

....
....
....

BUILT IN 1742

"THE CRADLE OF LIBERTY"

5.94

RESIDENTS IN 2010

WHAT DO BOSTONIANS PERCEIVE
IN THEIR DAILY LIFE?
HOW BIG BOSTON WOULD BE IN
THEIR SENSE?

?

0.000

VISITORS IN 2010

DO YOU THINK YOU HAVE SEEN
ALL PARTS OF BOSTON?
DO YOU KNOW BOSTON?

?

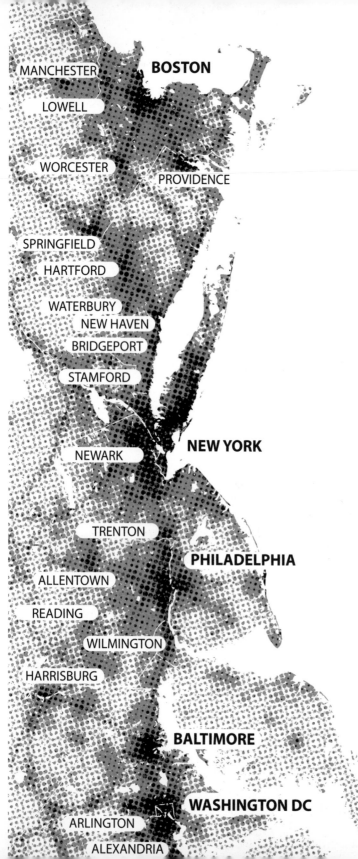

MANCHESTER

BOSTON

LOWELL

WORCESTER

PROVIDENCE

SPRINGFIELD

HARTFORD

WATERBURY

NEW HAVEN

BRIDGEPORT

STAMFORD

NEW YORK

NEWARK

TRENTON

PHILADELPHIA

ALLENTOWN

READING

WILMINGTON

HARRISBURG

BALTIMORE

WASHINGTON DC

ARLINGTON

ALEXANDRIA

BOSWASH

The term BosWash was first introduced by Hermut Kahn as a concept of having mega-metropolis that is formed from Boston in North to Washington to South. The idea comes from the urbanized pattern that a person can travel from Boston through New York to Washington without experiencing rural area. In BosWash, about 17% of the U.S population resides which is a bit less than 50 million people in a area of 137,000 km2. This megapolis, which is bigger than South Korea, produces 20% of the total U.S Gross Domestic Product, which puts it on fifth biggest GDP nations in the world next to Germany and ahead of France. Also, it is consisted with the most influential cities in the world in major field such as; financial field of New York, political influence of Washington and education of Boston.

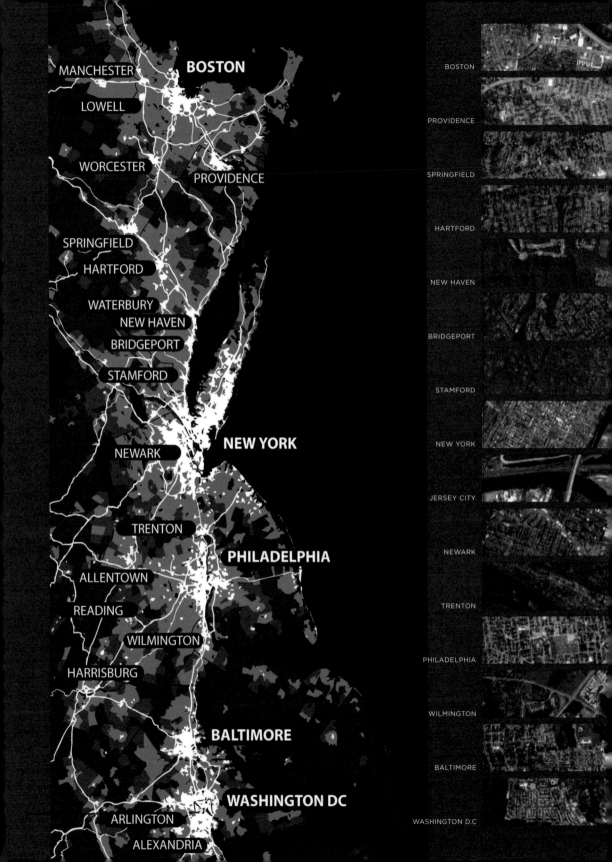

MANCHESTER

BOSTON

LOWELL

WORCESTER

PROVIDENCE

SPRINGFIELD

HARTFORD

WATERBURY

NEW HAVEN

BRIDGEPORT

STAMFORD

NEW YORK

NEWARK

TRENTON

PHILADELPHIA

ALLENTOWN

READING

WILMINGTON

HARRISBURG

BALTIMORE

WASHINGTON DC

ARLINGTON

ALEXANDRIA

BOSTON

PROVIDENCE

SPRINGFIELD

HARTFORD

NEW HAVEN

BRIDGEPORT

STAMFORD

NEW YORK

JERSEY CITY

NEWARK

TRENTON

PHILADELPHIA

WILMINGTON

BALTIMORE

WASHINGTON D.C

INNOVATIVE BOSTON

The analysts first named Boston as the second-top global innovation destination in 2007. In 2011, the analysts stated that Boston's dominant institutions Harvard and MIT, coupled with a strengthening start-up and arts in global networks kept the city number one overall globally across multiple economic segments in the turbulent national economic cycle.

-2thinknow press release-

TOP25 INNOVATION CITIES

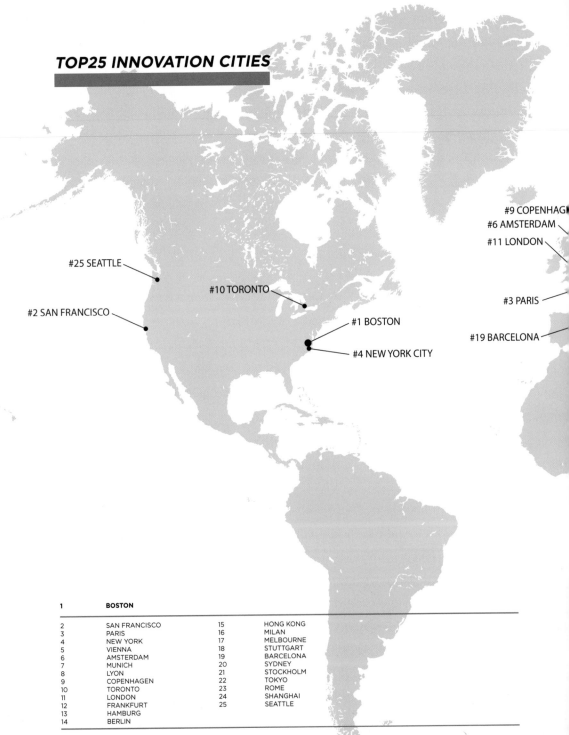

#9 COPENHAG[
#6 AMSTERDAM
#11 LONDON

#3 PARIS

#19 BARCELONA

#25 SEATTLE

#10 TORONTO

#2 SAN FRANCISCO

#1 BOSTON

#4 NEW YORK CITY

1	BOSTON		
2	SAN FRANCISCO	15	HONG KONG
3	PARIS	16	MILAN
4	NEW YORK	17	MELBOURNE
5	VIENNA	18	STUTTGART
6	AMSTERDAM	19	BARCELONA
7	MUNICH	20	SYDNEY
8	LYON	21	STOCKHOLM
9	COPENHAGEN	22	TOKYO
10	TORONTO	23	ROME
11	LONDON	24	SHANGHAI
12	FRANKFURT	25	SEATTLE
13	HAMBURG		
14	BERLIN		

Source: 2thinknow Innovation Cities™ Program: www.innovation-cities.com [or the link of the page you are referencing]

#21 STOCKHOLM
#13 HAMBURG
#14 BERLIN
#12 FRANKFURT
#5 VIENNA
#7 MUNICH
STUTTGART
ROME
MILAN

#22 TOKYO
#24 SHANGHAI
#15 HONG KONG

#20 SYDNY
#17 MELBOURNE

SOURCE: WWW.INNOVATION-CITIES.COM

FACEBOOK WAS FIST ESTABLISHED IN CAMBRIDGE, PART OF METROPOLITAN BOSTON, IN 2004 AND AS OF 2012, IT HAS MORE THAN 800 MILLION ACTIVE USERS. BUT IT IS NO LONGER LOCATED IN BOSTON AREA.

ipcar.com

ZIPCAR WAS FOUNDED IN CAMBRIDGE IN 2000, AND
NOW HAVE 650,000 MEMBERS AROUND 28 STATES AND
PROVINCES IN THE NATION

120
121

CITY OF FIRST

1632 The first windmill is built on Copp's Hill.   1632 The first public anti-smoking law is established.   1634 Boston Common becomes the first public park in America.   1635 Boston Latin School is established as the first public secondary school. It is still operating.   1639 Post Office, America's 1st (at Richard Fairbanks' House)   1639   UFO, America's First UFO Sighting 1653 Boston Public Library, America's 1st Public Library   1672 The first U.S. mail route is opened between Boston and New York.   1690 Paper Money, 1st (Issued When Government Was Insolvent) 1 7 0 4 The first regularly issued American newspaper The Boston News-Letter is published. 1714 The Union Oyster House opens. It is the oldest American restaurant still operating under the same name.   1716 The first American lighthouse is built in Boston Harbor.   1721 Inoculation, America's 1st (Smallpox) 1757   Human Flight, America's 1st by John Childs In Bird Suit   1765 The first chocolate factory Walter Baker Company is opened in Dorchester.   1770 British Concession, 1st (Withdraw Troops to Castle William)   1780 The first State Constitution is created. 1 7 8 4 The Bell in Hand Tavern opens. It is now known as the oldest pub in the U.S.   1785 Unitarian Church, America's 1st (King's Chapel)   1790 Circumnavigate Globe, America's 1st (Columbia)   1806 The first African-American meeting house is constructed. It is the country's oldest existing black church.   1816   Mutual Savings Bank, America's 1st (Provident)   1827 Francis Leiber opens the first swimming school and pool in America. Among the first students to enroll is John Quincy Adams.   1829 The first school for the blind is established as Perkins Institute.   1 8 3 1 The Liberator, 1st Radical Abolitionist Newspaper 1835 The first public school for African-American children, the Abiel Smith School, is opened. 1837 Samuel Morse invents the electric telegraph based on Morse Code, a simple pattern of dots and dashes.   1838 Boston becomes the first city to establish its own police department.   1845 Sewing Machine, Invented by Elias Howe   1846 Anesthetic, 1st Demonstration Ether (Mass General Hospital)

1848 The Boston Public Library becomes the first publicly supported free municipal library in the world. 1852 Electric Fire Alarm System (Telegraphy), 1st City To Utilize 1860 Aerial Photo, America's 1st from balloon by J. W. Black 1861 Black U.S. Federal Employee, 1st, William Nell (Post Office) 1862 Organized Football Club, America's 1st 1863 Mass 54th, 1st Civil War Free Black Regiment 1865 Robert Ware of M.I.T. begins the first professional training program for architects. 1875 Telephone, Invented by Alexander Graham Bell 1875 The first American Christmas card is printed by Louis Prang. 1876 The first telephone is demonstrated by Alexander Graham Bell in Boston. 1877 Helen Magill White graduates from Boston University and becomes the first woman in the United States to earn a Ph.D. 1879 Mary Baker Eddy founds the Church of Christ, Scientist in Boston. 1881 Boston YMCA staffer Robert J. Roberts coins the term "body building" and develops exercise classes that anticipate today's modern fitness workouts. 1896 Fannie Farmer publishes "The Boston Cooking-School Cook Book" – the first cookbook in America. Her cookbook provides scientific explanations of the chemical processes that occur in food during cooking and also helps to standardize the system of measurements. 1897 The Boston subway opens as the first underground metro in North America. Today it is affectionately known as the "T" and is run by the Massachusetts Bay Transportation Authority. 1901 Disposable Blade, Invented by K. Gillette & W. Nickerson 1903 The first modern World Series is played in Major League Baseball as the Boston Americans beat the Pittsburgh Pirates five games to three in a best of nine series. 1909 Off-Price Store, 1st, Filene's Basement 1924 Mutual Fund, 1st (L. Sherman Adams, Mass Investors Trust) 1928 MIT professor Vannevar Bush constructs a Differential Analyser, an analog computer that could solve differential equations with as many as 18 independent variables. This is one of the first advanced computing devices used for practial research. 1944 Harvard professor Howard Aiken develops the Automatic Sequence Controlled Calculator – the first automatic digital computer. 1954 Kidney Transplant, 1st Peter Bent Brigham Hospital)

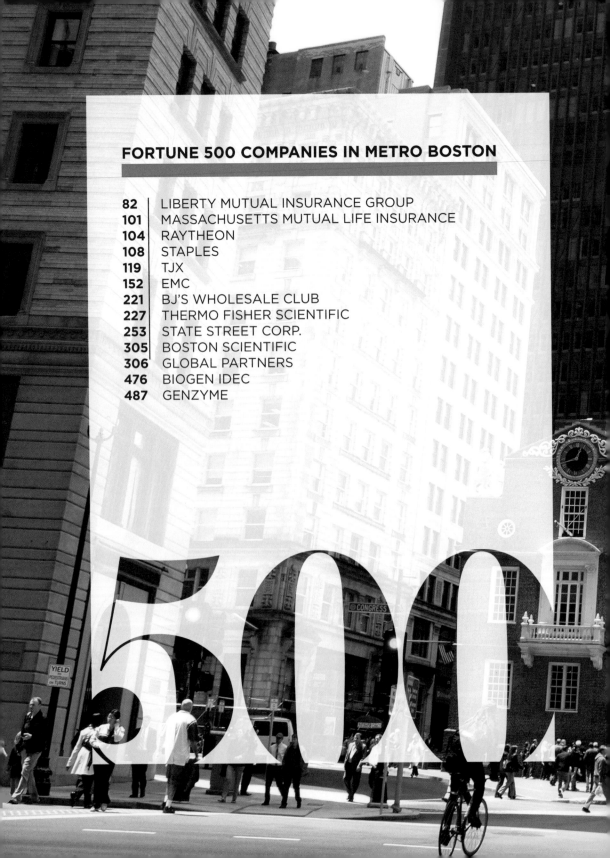

FORTUNE 500 COMPANIES IN METRO BOSTON

82	LIBERTY MUTUAL INSURANCE GROUP
101	MASSACHUSETTS MUTUAL LIFE INSURANCE
104	RAYTHEON
108	STAPLES
119	TJX
152	EMC
221	BJ'S WHOLESALE CLUB
227	THERMO FISHER SCIENTIFIC
253	STATE STREET CORP.
305	BOSTON SCIENTIFIC
306	GLOBAL PARTNERS
476	BIOGEN IDEC
487	GENZYME

The concept of URBAN CORE comes from the property of the core that gravitates urban activities in a city. It is where people gather for certain purpose and urban interactions happen. Addition to urban core, MULTIPLE CORE, a series of urban cores, only emerges in a city that can hold a variety of urban activities in larger scale, which can be understood as METROPOLITAN.

URBAN CORES

MULTIPLE-CORES

BY: DONGWOO YIM

Words like urban, metropolitan or cosmopolitan seem to be engaged the architectural field, but their use is not limited to this profession. They have rather become trendy words to explains certain aspects that describe city conditions. Perhaps, architects and urbanists tend to, or prefer to, define those words objectively with statical data such as population, density or area.

In the book "Metropolitan World Atlas", a number of metropolitan cities are introduced based on statistical data, including infrastructure and global networks. It is a very clear approach to explain what is urban, what is metropolitan, or what is cosmopolitan. However, being adjective words, they are subjective rather than objective, perceptive rather than statistical, and experiential rather than analytical.

The twenty-first century is a period of urban triumph. More than half of the world population is living in an urban setting, and more than 75% will live in a city by 2050. This implies that not only the number and size of cities are growing, but also there is a more ambiguous division between urban and rural. Many rural areas are turning into urban, including sub-urban, areas. But again, how do we define a city or urban area? By definition, urban area is an area with higher density, which is a very relative definition since it needs to be compared to something else; higher density than what other area? This is an indeterminate way for differentiating urban from rural when 50% of the global population is living in a "city". Then, are those cities all urban, metropolitan, or cosmopolitan? As mentioned in the beginning, perhaps we cannot say they are all "urban" based on the statistical facts.
For instance, San Jose, which is the third largest city in California, and the tenth in the U.S, is definitely a city with no doubt, and it even has a metropolitan area that extends to San Francisco and Oakland. However do most of people consider it as

WHEN THERE ARE MULTIPLE CORES IN A CITY, THE CITY PROVIDES THE PUBLIC MORE TO EXPERIENCE IN DIFFERENT PART OF THE CITY

"

urban or metropolitan? Perhaps not. It is mostly considered as Silicon Valley, the city of information technology. On the other hand, most of people conceive San Francisco as urban, if not metropolitan, even though it has less population and smaller size than San Jose. What makes them to be perceived differently? Perhaps, it is not just statistical data that makes them different.

Urban core is a perceptive way to understand a city. Core, by definition, is the most important part, or the central part, of something. In a way, this definition can also be adopted to a city regarding that core is the central part of the city where the city starts to expand. Also, it is true that in most traditional cities, the city center, is the most important part of the city, because it is where most of business, commercial, and civic functions are located. By seeing the core of the city, we get a sense of personality, or character to the city, which tells us how we perceive what "urban" is. In his book "The Image of the City," Kevin Lynch gives us clues for understanding a city by perceiving such elements like paths, landmarks, nodes, edges, and districts of a city. The perception of them forms the image of the city. The perception for a city being "urban" or "metropolitan" is very much related to what Lynch presents.

If we start understanding urban core as a perceptional concept, we can break the preconception of an urban core being attached to a location, and relate it to activity. An urban core can be explained with nodes and districts in a way that as a node, an urban core represents the points of intense activities, and as a district it represents a certain section of the city. Therefore, an urban core is where urban activities happen, no matter where it is located in the city, and is an element that forms the image of the city as well. It is the node, or district that gravitates people, whether they are local or visitors, and generates activities.

However, the importance in meaning from the term, "urban core," comes from the word "urban" rather than "core." It is "urban" that implies interactions, not just between people, but between city elements. For instance, Disney World can be considered a large core of Orlando in the sense that it attracts more than 16 million visitors a year, but can we say Disney World is an urban core just because of the fact that it gravitates people? Probably not. Although it attracts millions to a specific location inside the city, it lacks an interaction between the node and the city. It acts as an island of activity. In fact, that is why theme parks, company campuses and shopping malls are planned as generators of suburban development, not the result of urbanity, and do not necessarily need to be part of the larger urban setting. The interactions should also happen in morphological forms. Since urban cores are the result of urbanity, urban cores should be dissolved into the city fabric. Going back to Lynch's argument, nodes and districts are not alien elements, but regular element in the city that are perceived in certain way. We are trying to see urban cores not based on functions, or programs, but based on their responds to the urban setting. Therefore, depending on its morphological form, an institution in a city can be an urban core, or not. If the institution has a certain periphery that separates itself from the city fabric, it is hard to understand it as an urban core in a way that there is a clear limit in terms of interaction. On the other hand, if an institution mutates its physical forms to be dissolved into the fabric, this is the moment when it starts to interact with the city and generate urban activities.

Then the question is, where are urban cores located in a city? Traditionally, urban cores can be associated with a city center. However, as a city grows, it required more nodes that can be multiple centers of different areas. Sometimes, they are understood as satellite districts that function similarly as the city center. However, for the purpose of this research, we call them multi-cores rather than satellites, because there is no hierarchical distinction. In a way, a multi-core city functions like a galaxy rather than a solar system, differentiating a single core city from a multi-core city.

A single core city has a very clear city center that houses most of civic functions, as well as businesses, and cultural facilities. Most cases, the size of the city only permits one core. The size limits the capacity for multiple cores. Campus towns or company towns like Ann Arbor or Pontiac City, tend to have only one core. And perhaps, we do not consider those cities as "urban", not even close to "metropolitan". It seems the perception of "urban" comes from depth of urban experiences we get from a city, which mostly relate to core activities. Therefore, it is very hard to expect deep layers of urban experiences when there is only a single core in the city.

On the other hand, when there are multiple cores in a city, the city provides the public more to experience in different part of the city. As mentioned above, the city exists like a galaxy and cannot be explained, or understood by one specific part of the city. We cannot understand New York City through only seeing Times Square, nor can we pick one major part of Shanghai that explains the whole city. Those cities are understood only through multiple cores, and the depth and active atmosphere of multiple cores let people think those cites are "urban" or "metropolitan." For instance, Shinjuku Station in Tokyo is conceived as a transportation hub as well as a highly commercialized district, while Nihonbashi is well known as a financial district. Hence, the activities and ambiance you experience at Shinjuku Station will be different from Nihonbashi. This variation gives a depth of urban activities to the city, and this is the moment when people perceive "urban," and "metropolitan." This is a clue to the question of why San Jose is perceived differently from San Francisco even though it is bigger in size and in population.

AFTER ALL, DIFFERENT CORES GRAVITATE PEOPLE FOR DIFFERENT REASONS. IN THIS RESEARCH, WE HAVE DESCRIBED CORES IN BOSTON UNDER SEVEN DIFFERENT CATEGORIES; TRANSIT CORE, INDUSTRIAL CORE, COMMERCIAL CORE, INSTITUTIONAL CORE, CULTURAL CORE, ATHLETIC CORE, AND TEMPORARY CORE.

"

In short, no matter what the definition of metropolis, or metropolitan is, it seems very clear that metropolitan, as an adjective word, comes from experience of a city through multiple cores. Then the question is whether only a metropolis would have multiple cores that let people conceive the city as metropolitan. All metropolises have multiple cores, but perhaps not all cities that have multiple cores are metropolises. But at least those cities will be conceived as cities that have metropolitan features. Boston is a very good example of this relationship between metropolis, metropolitan and multiple cores. As described above, cities like New York, Shanghai, and Tokyo cannot be understood by a single core in the city. Similarly, we cannot describe Boston based on a certain district of the city. Perhaps what tourists experience in the city is different from what students in Boston perceive. For instance, when you ask students from Harvard University about their experience of Boston, they will most likely describe activities around Harvard Square, and not around the central part of Boston. And it is very likely that they rarely venture outside that area. On the other hand, tourists in Boston, who mostly follow the Freedom Trail, understand the city through the trail, never knowing other parts like Fenway Park where three million local people visit a year.

After all, different cores gravitate people for different reasons. In this research, we have described cores in Boston under seven different categories; transit core, industrial core, commercial core, institutional core, cultural core, athletic core, and temporary core. We can understand the metropolitan qualities of Boston through the analysis of these cores. Perhaps, this could also explain why Boston is conceived as more "urban," or even "metropolitan" than cities like Detroit, or Baltimore.

TRANSIT
CORES

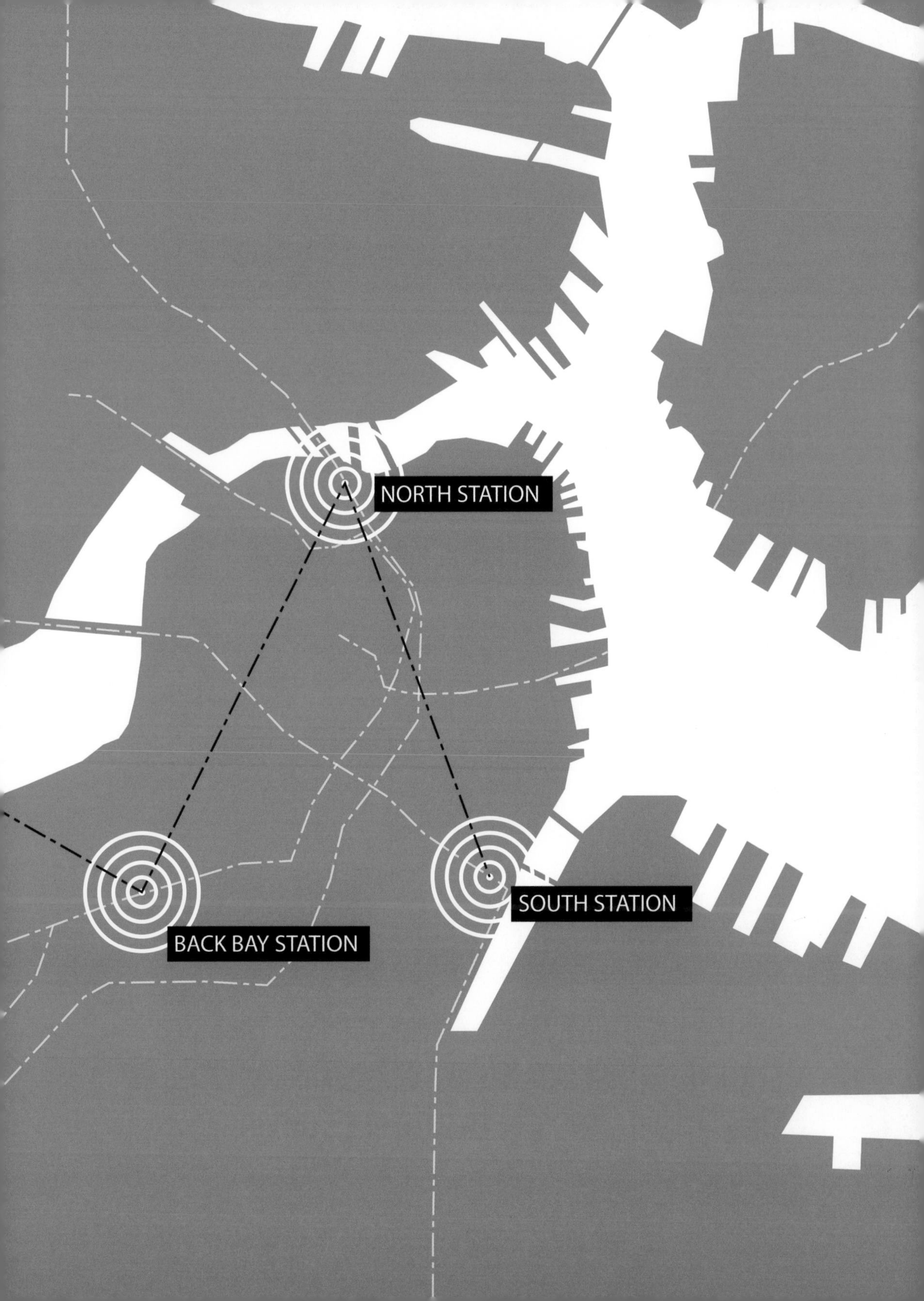

NORTH STATION

BACK BAY STATION

SOUTH STATION

" **BOSTON HAS THREE MAJOR COMMUTER RAIL TRANSIT STATIONS WITHIN 1KM RADIUS, WHILE MOST OF CITIES IN SIMILAR SCALE ARE SERVED WITH ONE STATION.**

2,174,000

TOTAL NUMBER OF PASSENGER

- -

TOTAL NUMBER OF PLATFORMS

 6TH

SOUTH STATION, 6TH THE MOST
**BUSIEST TRANSIT
STATION IN THE US**

30

MAXIMUM DISTANCE
BETWEEN STATIONS

2KM

TOTAL
#OF
TRACKS

STATION	PASSENGERS
NEW YORK, NY	8,377,944
WASHINGTON, DC	4,572,878
PHILADELPHIA, PA	3,787,331
CHICAGO, IL	3,288,054
LOS ANGELES, CA	1,517,342
BOSTON SOUTH STATION, MA	1,311,205
SACRAMENTO, CA	1,107,220
BALTIMORE, MD	926,245
ALBANY-RENSSELAER, NY	737,259
NEW HAVEN, CT	723,287
SAN DIEGO, CA	715,043
WILMINGTON, DE	680,079
SEATTLE, WA	677,953
PORTLAND, OR	672,608
NEWARK, NJ	658,089
BWI AIRPORT, MD	654,151
IRVINE, CA	630,190
PROVIDENCE, RI	602,474
MILWAUKEE, WI	588,617
HARRISBURG, PA	547,257
EMERYVILLE, CA	529,965
LANCASTER, PA	514,971
BOSTON BACK BAY, MA	495,074
TRENTON, NJ	420,533
BOSTON NORTH STATION, MA	418,993

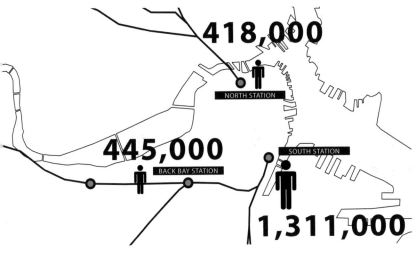

Riders per year : All three commuter rails stations in Boston are ranked in top 25 stations by ridership in the nation.

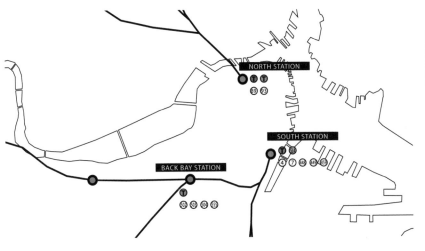

Connections : They are located at the periphery of central Boston and are connected through MBTA to the center.

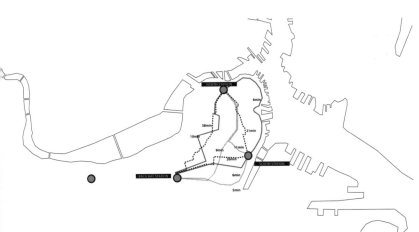

Distances : All stations are located very close to each other, and they can be reached by MBTA subway within 11 minutes from one to another.

	SOUTH STATION	NORTH STATION	BACK BAY STATION

PASSENGERS/YEAR

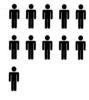

TRACK

PLATFORM

RAIL LINES

SUBWAY CONNECTION

BUS CONNECTION

BUS LINES

WATER TAXI

MAJOR FACILITIES NEAR STATIONS

PAUL REVERE PARK
MUSEUM OF SCIENCE
NASHUA STREET PARK
NORTH STATION T
PORTAL PARK
ROSE KENNEDY GREENWAY
US SOCIAL SECURITY ADMINISTRATION
CHARLESBANK PLAY GROUND
NORTH END BRANCH LIBRARY
GOVERNMENT CENTER PARKING GARAGE
MASS. GENERAL HOSPITAL
FANUEIL HALL MARKET PLACE
GOVERNMENT CENTER
GOVERNMENT CENTER STATION
NEW ENGLAND AQUARIUM
SOUTH STATION
AQUARIUM STATION
POST OFFICE SQUARE
WHARF DISTRICT PARK
DOWNTOWN CROSSING STATION
US COURTHOUSE
BOSTON COMMON
DEWEY SQUARE
LEATHER DISTRICT PARK
CHINATOWN STATION T
CHINATOWN PARK
BOSTON CHIDREN'S MUSEUM
ARLINGTON STATION T
TUFTS MEDICAL STATION T
COPLEY SQUARE STATION T
SOUTH BOSTON POSTAL ANNEX
COPLEY SQUARE
BOSTON PUBLIC LIBRARY
JOHN HANCOCK TOWER
HYNES CONVENTION CENTER
BOSTON CONVENTION EXHIBITION CENTER
PRUDENTIAL MALL
PRUDENTIAL CENTER
PRUDENTIAL STATION T
GILLETTE WORLD HEADQUATERS
CHRISTIAN SCIENCE MOTHER CHURCH
PUBLIC GARDEN

INDUSTI
CORES

KENDALL SQ

LONGWOOD MEDICAL CENTER

FINANCIAL DISTRICT

OSTON HAS THE BEST BIO-TECHNOLOGY INDUSTRY IN THE
VORLD TOGETHER WITH THE BEST MEDICAL FACILITIES, AND
S THE FIRST CITY TO ESTABLISH A MUTUAL FUND.

BIOTECHNOLOGY COMPANIES

15 PER ACRE,
KENDALL SQUARE

SKYSCRAPERS IN BOSTON LOCATED IN FINANCIAL DISTRICT

80%

NUMBER OF FINANCIAL SERVICES PER ACRE, FINANCIAL DISTRICT

4.6

250 (VERBAL EMPLOYEES PER ACRE)

KENDALL SQUARE

10
ACRE

150
NUMBER OF BIOTECHNOLOGY COMPANY

729
NUMBER OF

"Why Cambridge?" asked Dr. Daniel Vasella, chairman and CEO of Novartis AG in a Monday news conference at MIT. "Analysis shows that it is more and more difficult to attract and retain scientific talent, so we have to go where the talent is. Cambridge is a pool of scientific talent not found elsewhere in the world."

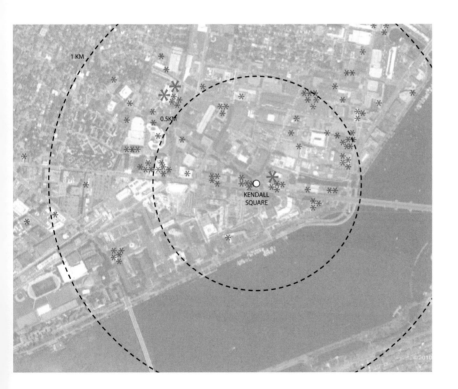

Located in Cambridge, Massachusetts, Kendall Square is the globe's leading innovation district. With MIT at its core and Harvard within walking distance, Kendall Square has a 200-year heritage of fostering the kinds of ideas that change the world. It is home to brilliant minds, dreamers and hard workers.

LONGWOOD MEDICAL AREA

43,600
EMPLOYEE

1,200
NEW JOBS PER YEAR

8,800
JOB OPENINGS PER YEAR

175
ACRE

Boston's Longwood Medical and Academic area (LMA) is a thriving community of medical, academic, research, and cultural organizations that combine to create a powerful economic engine for the city and the state. *MASCO (Medical Academic and Scientific Community Organization)

Nearly 92% of LMA employees work for health care and research institutions. Fifteen percent of these workers are researchers. There are approximately 10,000 researchers in the LMA if you include those paid by grants, or otherwise supported by 2 non-pay-roll sources. There are approximately 1,800 physicians and dentists, 1,700 residents/interns and nearly 7,000 registered and vocational nurses on payroll.

*MASCO (Medical Academic and Scientific Community Organization)

30,000 TOTAL NUMBER OF JOBS PROVIDED
14 NUMBER OF INSTITUTION
1,300,600 TOTAL AMOUNT OF FLOOR AREA IN SQUARE METER

FINANCIAL DISTRICT

61
ACRE

283
FINANCIAL SERVICES

3,921
PROFESSIONAL SERVICES

77
REAL ESTATE SERVICES

Financial District

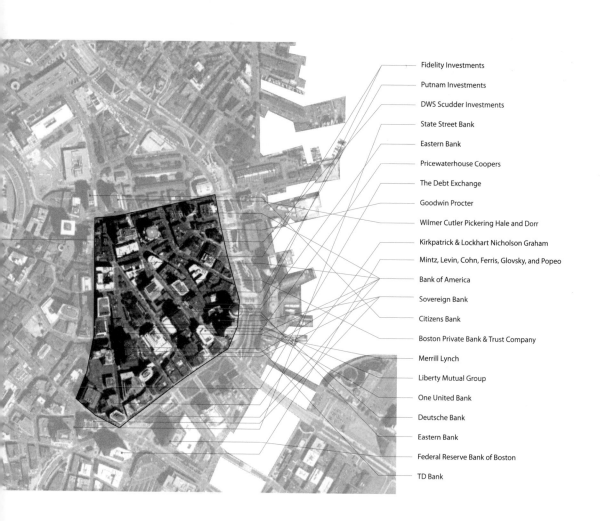

Fidelity Investments

Putnam Investments

DWS Scudder Investments

State Street Bank

Eastern Bank

Pricewaterhouse Coopers

The Debt Exchange

Goodwin Procter

Wilmer Cutler Pickering Hale and Dorr

Kirkpatrick & Lockhart Nicholson Graham

Mintz, Levin, Cohn, Ferris, Glovsky, and Popeo

Bank of America

Sovereign Bank

Citizens Bank

Boston Private Bank & Trust Company

Merrill Lynch

Liberty Mutual Group

One United Bank

Deutsche Bank

Eastern Bank

Federal Reserve Bank of Boston

TD Bank

6/11 PROPOSED SKYSCRAPER IN FINANCIAL
21/26 SKYSCRAPER IN FINANCIAL DISTRICT OUT OF TOTAL

COMME
CORES

CIAL

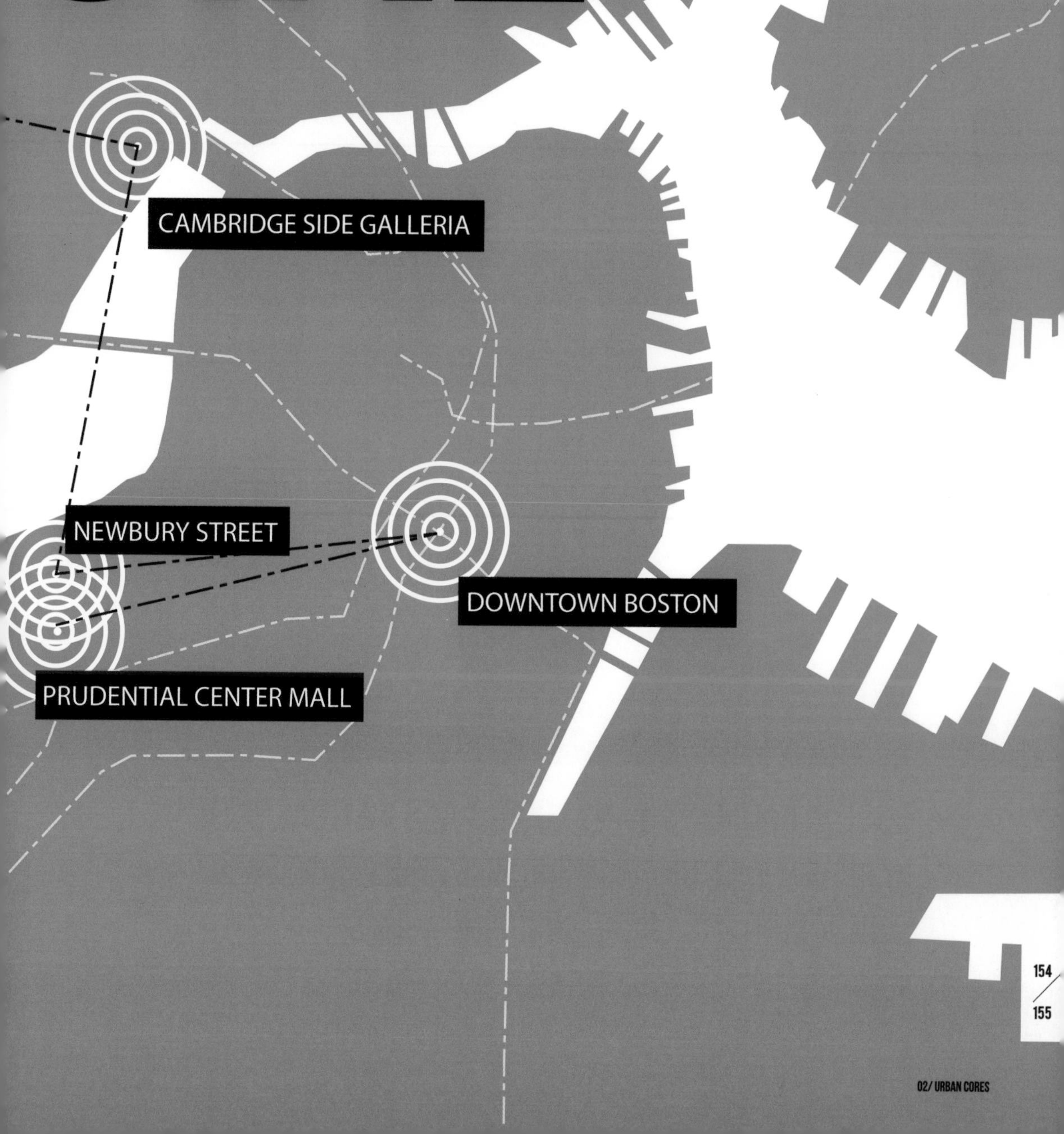

CAMBRIDGE SIDE GALLERIA

NEWBURY STREET

DOWNTOWN BOSTON

PRUDENTIAL CENTER MALL

" BOSTON ATTRACTS MANY LOCALS AND VISITORS WITH VARIOUS TYPES OF COMMERCIAL STORES FROM SMALL STOREFRONTS TO LARGE SHOPPING MALLS.

RN

STORES PER KM,
@ NEWBURY STREET

185

RETAIL
STORES
@
PRUDENTIAL
MALL

+

COPLEY
PLAZA MALL

PEDESTRIAN
PER DAY
@ DOWNTOWN
CROSSING

230,000

FAR=3 (GALLERIA MALL)

NEWBURY STREET

236

NUMBER OF RETAIL STORES

80

RETAIL STORE PER KM

It is one of the most famous touristic destination in Boston that is located in the Back Bay. Newbury Street develops its own very distinctive and appealing character and becomes one of the nicest shopping streets in Boston, or anywhere. Renovated town houses with large glass bays on the ground floor produce a delightful urban landscape....

*Donlyn Lyndon

COMMERCIAL TYPICAL TYPE

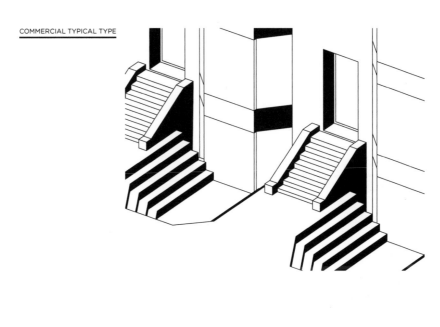

NEWBURY STREET SECTION

DOWNTOWN CROSSING

230,000
PEDESTRIANS PER DAY

165,000
OFFICE WORKERS

1,800
HOTEL ROOMS

4,710
NUMBER OF BUSINESS

It is located between Boston Common and Financial District in central Boston. The area was first developed as hub of department store in early 20th century. In 2006, the Filene's Basement was closed and the site is remained as empty with a huge hole until now. Also, Borders, another landmark of the area, closed its business in 2011. Most of retail stores are located on Washington Street, the major street of the area, and it is pedestrian-only in Downtown Crossing area.

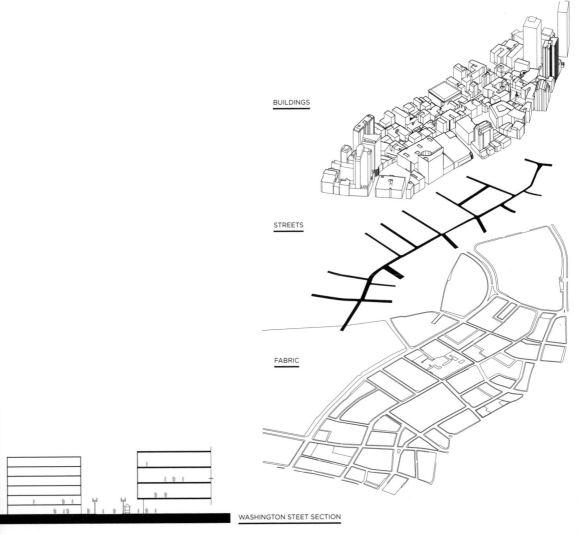

BUILDINGS

STREETS

FABRIC

WASHINGTON STEET SECTION

PRUDENTIAL MALL & COPLEY MALL

60,000

PEDESTRIANS PASSING THROUGH PER DAY

55,000

WORKERS IN 2 BLOCK RADIUS

Both of them are enclosed shopping mall in Back Bay area that are connected to each other and developed as part of Prudential Center Development. Since they opened the business in the 1980s and the 1990s, they became a new type of shopping mall and strip in the city. The shopping strip not only for retails attached but also connections to existing urban fabrics nearby.

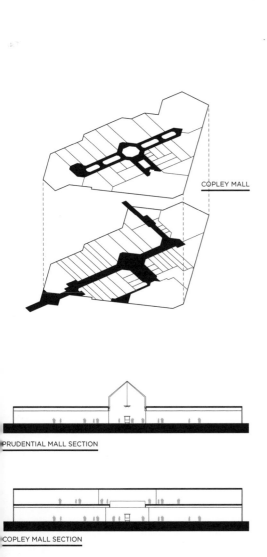

PRUDENTIAL

COPLEY MALL

PRUDENTIAL MALL SECTION

COPLEY MALL SECTION

02/ URBAN CORES

GALLERIA MALL

133
TOTAL NUMBER OF RETAIL STORES

4
ANCHORING DEPARTMENT STORE

93,000
RETAIL AREA IN SQUARE METER

It is located in Cambridge offering more than 130 retail stores with four department stores. It was first opened in 1990 as part of the 1978 East Cambridge Riverfront Plan. Just as Copley Place and Prudential Mall, Cambridgeside Galleria can be accessed very easily by public transportation system, MBTA, and it is the only shopping mall/or area that can be reached by boat in Boston.

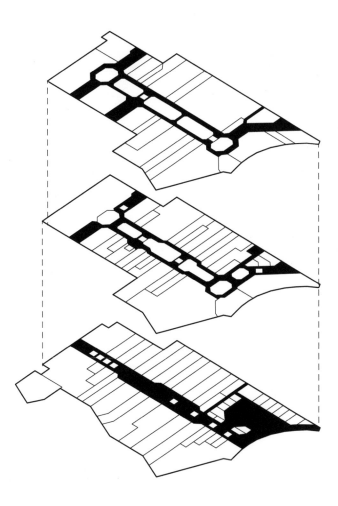

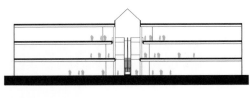

GALLERIA MALL SECTION

INSTITU CORES

BOSTON UNIVERSITY

NORTHEASTERN UNIVERSITY

IONAL

SUFFOLK UNIVERSITY

EMERSON COLLEGE

" **BOSTON HAS THE MOST NUMBER OF INSTITUTIONS AND STUDENTS PER CAPITA IN THE WORLD. BOSTON NEVER CAN BE EXPLAINED WITH OUT INSTITUTIONS.**

35

IN ADMINISTRATIVE BOSTON

25%

OF POPULATION IN BOSTON IS

STUDENT

8

NUMBER OF UNIVERSITIES OVER TEN-THOUSANDS OF STUDENTS

54

HIGHER EDUCATION IN INSTITUTIONS IN METROPOLITAN BOSTON

METROPOLITAN BOSTON

ANDOVER NEWTON THEOLOGICAL SCHOOL 350
BAY STATE COLLEGE 354
BENJAMIN FRANKLIN INSTITUTE OF TECHNOLOGY 513
BENTLY UNIVERSITY 5,662
BERKLEE COLLEGE OF MUSIC 4,054
BOSTON ARCHITECTURAL COLLEGE 1,338
BOSTON BAPTIST COLLEGE 153
BOSTON COLLEGE 14,621
BOSTON CONSERVATORY 613
BOSTON GRADUATE SCHOOL OF PSYCHOANALYSIS 178
BOSTON UNIVERSITY 31,766
BRANDEIS UNIVERSITY 5,327
BUNKER HILL COMMUNITY COLLEGE 8,806
CAMBRIDGE COLLEGE 5,355
CURRY COLLEGE 3,097
EASTERN NAZARENE COLLEGE 1,050
EMERSON COLLEGE 4,536
EMMANUEL COLLEGE 2,467
EPISCOPAL DIVINITY SCHOOL 108
FISHER COLLEGE 1,225
HARVARD UNIVERSITY 25,690
HEBREW COLLEGE 201
HELLENIC COLLEGE AND HOLY CROSS GREEK ORTHODOX
SCHOOL OF THEOLOGY 186
HULT INTERNATIONAL BUSINESS SCHOOL 1,000
LABOURE COLLEGE 548
LASELL COLLEGE 1,469
LESLEY UNIVERSITY 7,003
LONGY SCHOOL OF MUSIC 235
MASSACHUSETTS COLLEGE OF ART AND DESIGN 2,349
MASSACHUSETTS COLLEGE OF PHARMACY AND HEALTH SCI-
ENCES 3,909
MASSACHUSETTS INSTITUTE OF TECHNOLOGY 10,229
MASSACHUSETTS SCHOOL OF PROFESSIONAL PSYCHOLOGY 304
MGH INSTITUTE OF HEALTH PROFESSIONS 835
MOUNT IDA COLLEGE 1,460
NEW ENGLAND COLLEGE OF BUSINESS AND FINANCE 711
NEW ENGLAND COLLEGE OF OPTOMETRY 464
NEW ENGLAND CONSERVATORY 714
NEW ENGLAND INSTITUTE OF ART 1,975
NEW ENGLAND SCHOOL OF LAW 1,103
NEW ENGLAND SCHOOL OF PHOTOGRAPHY 119
NEWBURY COLLEGE 1,088
NORTHEASTERN UNIVERSITY 24,434
PINE MANOR COLLEGE 452
QUINCY COLLEGE 3,932
ROXBURY COMMUNITY COLLEGE 2,398
SAINT JOHN'S SEMINARY 118
SCHOOL OF THE MUSEUM OF FINE ARTS 797
SIMMONS COLLEGE 4,933
SUFFOLK UNIVERSITY 16,095
TUFTS UNIVERSITY 10,252
UNIVERSITY OF MASSACHUSETTS BOSTON 14,117
URBAN COLLEGE OF BOSTON 673
WENTWORTH ISNTITUTE OF TECHNOLOGY 3,816
WHEELOCK COLLEGE 1,109

236,291

STUDENTS

BOSTON PROPER

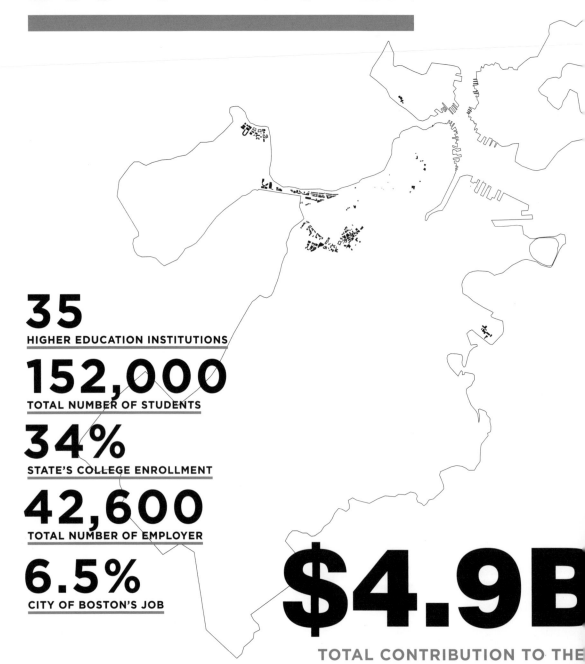

35
HIGHER EDUCATION INSTITUTIONS

152,000
TOTAL NUMBER OF STUDENTS

34%
STATE'S COLLEGE ENROLLMENT

42,600
TOTAL NUMBER OF EMPLOYER

6.5%
CITY OF BOSTON'S JOB

$4.9B
TOTAL CONTRIBUTION TO THE
GROSS CITY PRODUCT

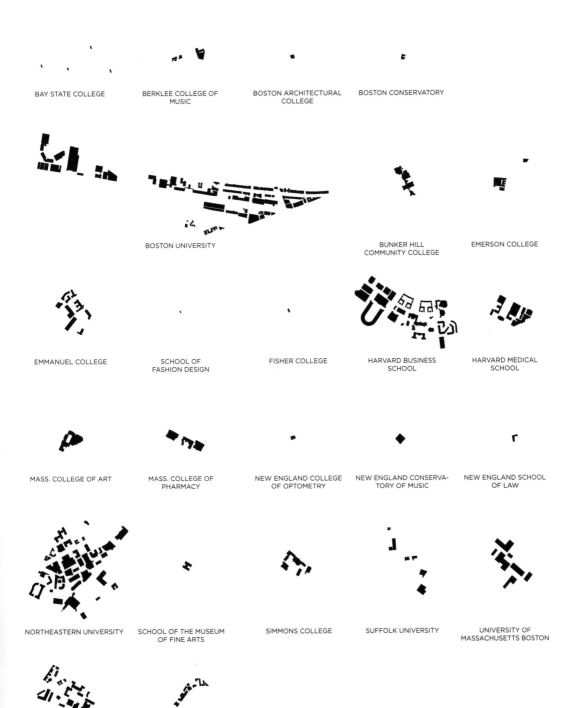

BAY STATE COLLEGE

BERKLEE COLLEGE OF MUSIC

BOSTON ARCHITECTURAL COLLEGE

BOSTON CONSERVATORY

BOSTON UNIVERSITY

BUNKER HILL COMMUNITY COLLEGE

EMERSON COLLEGE

EMMANUEL COLLEGE

SCHOOL OF FASHION DESIGN

FISHER COLLEGE

HARVARD BUSINESS SCHOOL

HARVARD MEDICAL SCHOOL

MASS. COLLEGE OF ART

MASS. COLLEGE OF PHARMACY

NEW ENGLAND COLLEGE OF OPTOMETRY

NEW ENGLAND CONSERVA-TORY OF MUSIC

NEW ENGLAND SCHOOL OF LAW

NORTHEASTERN UNIVERSITY

SCHOOL OF THE MUSEUM OF FINE ARTS

SIMMONS COLLEGE

SUFFOLK UNIVERSITY

UNIVERSITY OF MASSACHUSETTS BOSTON

WENTWORTH INSTITUTE OF TECHNOLOGY

WHEELOCK COLLEGE

Unlike generic institutional campus, urban campus is such a type that has a correlation to urban setting. Each urban campus develops its own strategy to build up the relationship and enhance the interaction. Thus, an urban campus becomes a core in a city instead of an island where interaction happens between campus and the city.

URBAN CAMPUS

CAMPUS IN CITY

URBAN CAMPUS CASE ONE

COLLEGES OF THE FENWAY

We believe that by working together we can enhance the student and faculty environments of our individual institutions while retaining the unique and special qualities of each of our schools.

Moreover, we believe that through the economic benefits of collaboration we can slow down the escalating costs of higher education through the sharing of resources, the ending of costly duplication, and the advantages of joint purchasing.

Through collaboration, our students and faculty will be able to share the best of both worlds: continuing to study, live, and teach in a small college environment while also enjoying the resources of a major academic environment.

Therefore, Emmanuel College, Massachusetts College of Art and Design, Massachusetts College of Pharmacy and Health Sciences, Simmons College, Wentworth Institute of Technology, and Wheelock College agree to form the Colleges of the Fenway.

* Principals of Collaboration, Colleges of the Fenway

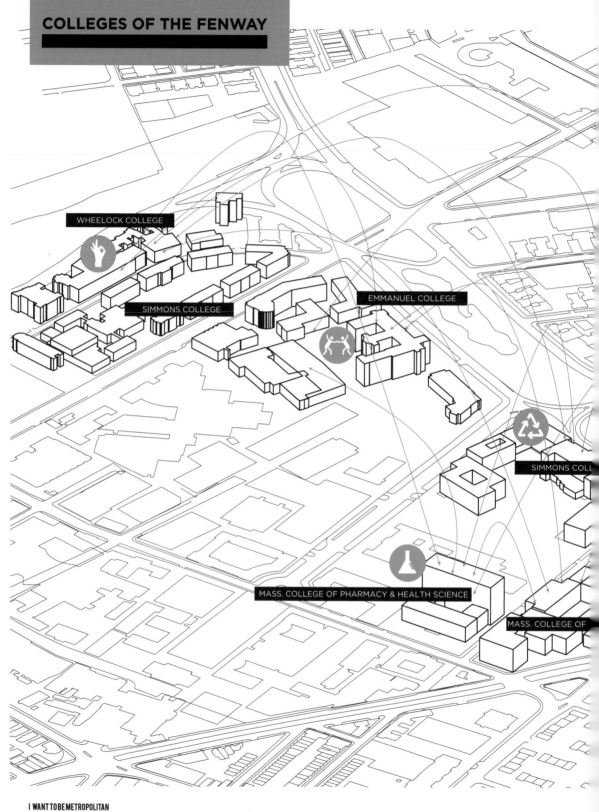

COLLEGES OF THE FENWAY

WHEELOCK COLLEGE

SIMMONS COLLEGE

EMMANUEL COLLEGE

SIMMONS COLL

MASS. COLLEGE OF PHARMACY & HEALTH SCIENCE

MASS. COLLEGE OF

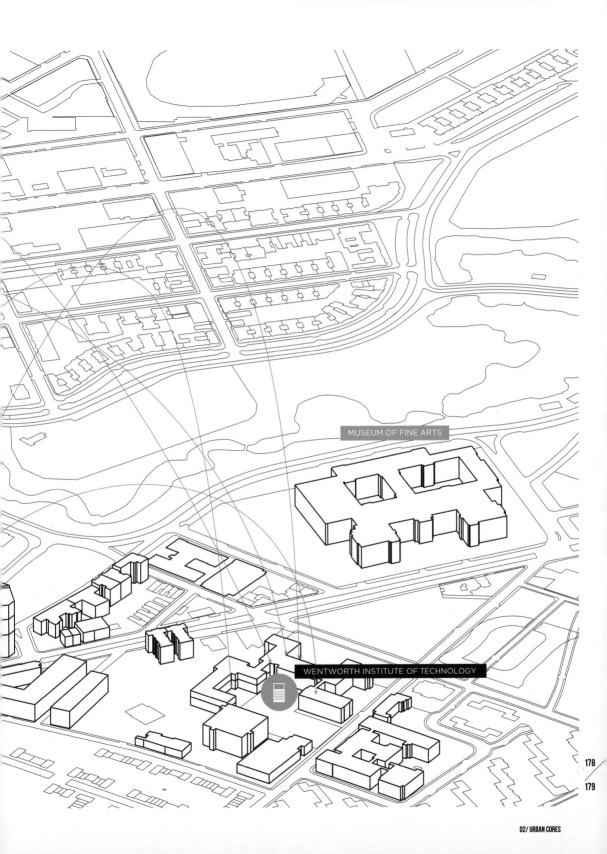

MUSEUM OF FINE ARTS

WENTWORTH INSTITUTE OF TECHNOLOGY

16.2%

TOTAL STUDENT POPULATION OF BOSTON

12,000
TOTAL NUMBER OF UNDERGRADUATE STUDENTS

6,500
TOTAL NUMBER OF GRADUATE STUDENTS

2,300
TOTAL NUMBER OF COURSES OFFERED

1,200 TOTAL NUMBER OF CROSS-REGISTER COURSES

225 CLUBS ON SIX CAMPUSES

2,868
FACULTY & STAFF MEMBERS

URBAN CAMPUS CASE TWO

EMERSON COLLEGE

Emerson College is located in the one of the oldest and most picturesque cities in America—and one of the best college towns in the country. Small in scale yet large in scope, the city is an internationally renowned center of excellence in higher education, healthcare, and technological innovation that attracts a diverse mix of students and professionals from around the world.

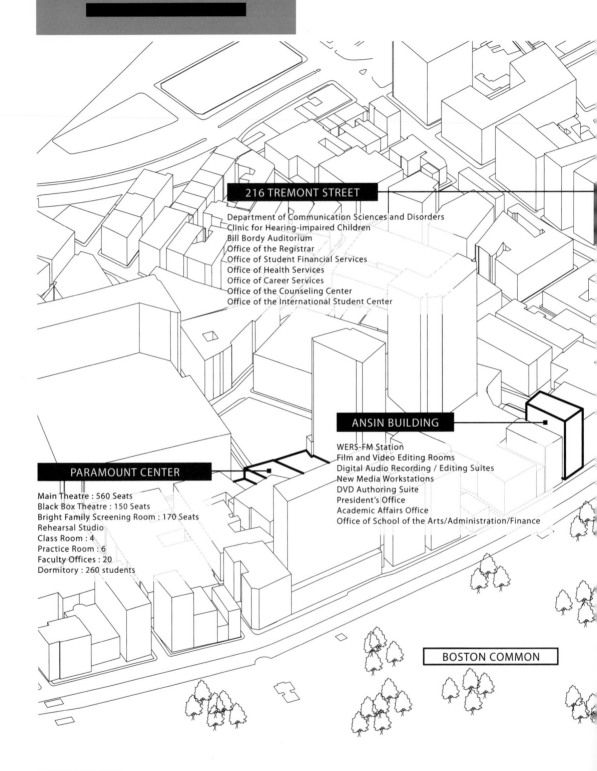

EMERSON COLLEGE

216 TREMONT STREET

Department of Communication Sciences and Disorders
Clinic for Hearing-impaired Children
Bill Bordy Auditorium
Office of the Registrar
Office of Student Financial Services
Office of Health Services
Office of Career Services
Office of the Counseling Center
Office of the International Student Center

ANSIN BUILDING

WERS-FM Station
Film and Video Editing Rooms
Digital Audio Recording / Editing Suites
New Media Workstations
DVD Authoring Suite
President's Office
Academic Affairs Office
Office of School of the Arts/Administration/Finance

PARAMOUNT CENTER

Main Theatre : 560 Seats
Black Box Theatre : 150 Seats
Bright Family Screening Room : 170 Seats
Rehearsal Studio
Class Room : 4
Practice Room : 6
Faculty Offices : 20
Dormitory : 260 students

BOSTON COMMON

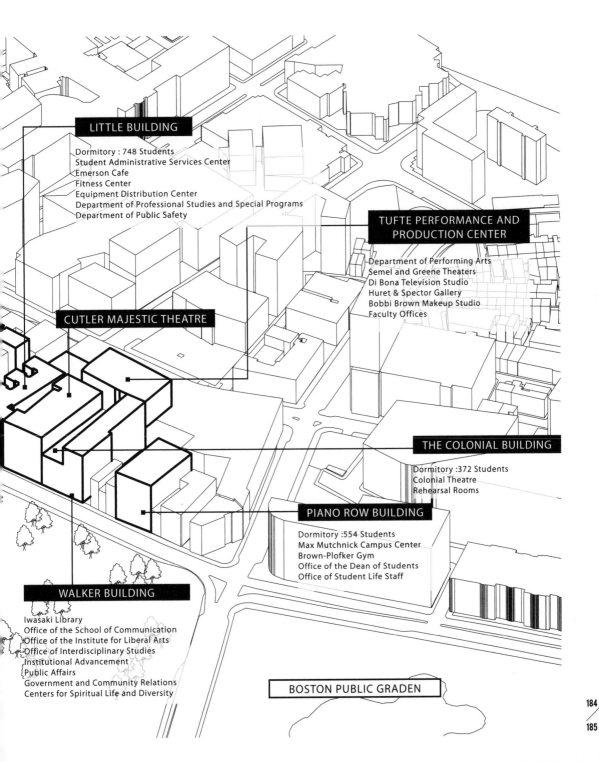

LITTLE BUILDING

Dormitory : 748 Students
Student Administrative Services Center
Emerson Cafe
Fitness Center
Equipment Distribution Center
Department of Professional Studies and Special Programs
Department of Public Safety

TUFTE PERFORMANCE AND PRODUCTION CENTER

Department of Performing Arts
Semel and Greene Theaters
Di Bona Television Studio
Huret & Spector Gallery
Bobbi Brown Makeup Studio
Faculty Offices

CUTLER MAJESTIC THEATRE

THE COLONIAL BUILDING

Dormitory :372 Students
Colonial Theatre
Rehearsal Rooms

PIANO ROW BUILDING

Dormitory :554 Students
Max Mutchnick Campus Center
Brown-Plofker Gym
Office of the Dean of Students
Office of Student Life Staff

WALKER BUILDING

Iwasaki Library
Office of the School of Communication
Office of the Institute for Liberal Arts
Office of Interdisciplinary Studies
Institutional Advancement
Public Affairs
Government and Community Relations
Centers for Spiritual Life and Diversity

BOSTON PUBLIC GRADEN

CULTUR
CORES

HARVARD SQUARE

NORTH END

FANEUIL HALL MARKETPLACE

CHINATOWN

" **BOSTON CANNOT BE EXPLAINED WITHOUT ITS VARIOUS CULTURES, AND MANY CULTURAL NEIGHBORHOODS, THERE ARE FOUR MAJOR AREAS THAT CONTAIN BOTH CULTURAL AND HISTORICAL VALUE OF THE CITY.**

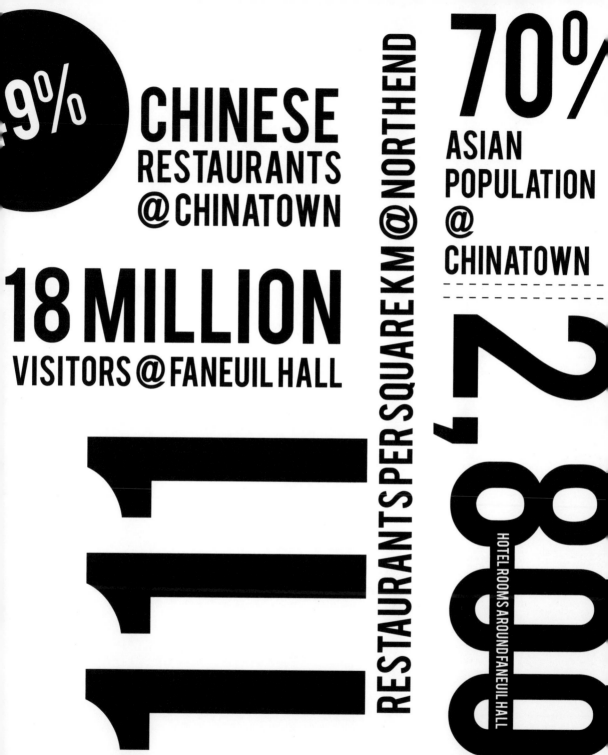

49%

CHINESE
RESTAURANTS
@ CHINATOWN

70%
ASIAN
POPULATION
@
CHINATOWN

RESTAURANTS PER SQUARE KM @ NORTHEND

18 MILLION
VISITORS @ FANEUIL HALL

11

2,800

HOTEL ROOMS AROUND FANEUIL HALL

MILLION (VISITORS @ HARVARD SQUARE)

HARVARD SQUARE

CULTURAL CORE CASE ONE

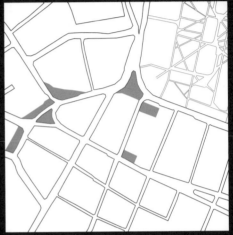

Harvard Square is one of the most popular touristic destination in Boston area with 8 millions visitors a year. It is formed with Harvard University campus, and offers various retails with 40 cultural organizations. For Harvard students, the square is what they conceive as "Boston".

NORTH END

CULTURAL CORE CASE TWO

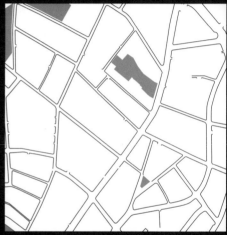

CHINATOWN

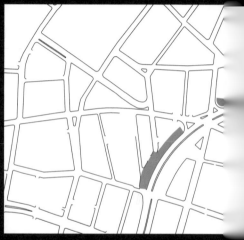

As many other cities in the world, Boston also has Chinatown in downtown of the city, and it is the center of Chinese culture. Nearly 70% of

FANEUILHALL HALL MARKETPLACE

CULTURAL CORE CASE FOUR

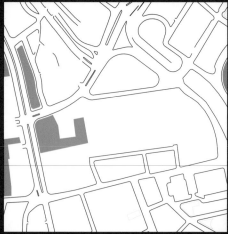

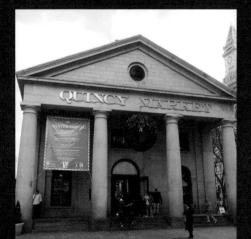

It is the area when the United States proclaimed itself as "The Cradle of Liberty" in 1742, and the major renovation took in place in 1976 as one of the first urban renewal project. Now it attracts 18 million visitors a year, the fifth most visited destination of the nation, with 150,000 workers in 500 meter radius.

ATHLET CORES

FENWAY PARK

TD GARDEN

OUT OF FOUR MAJOR PROFESSIONAL SPORTS IN THE U.S,
BOSTON HAS THREE MAJOR SPORTS FACILITIES IN TOWN;
FENWAY PARK FOR BASEBALL, TD GARDEN FOR BASKETBALL
AND ICE HOCKEY.

2ND HIGHEST OCCUPANCY RATE @ FENWAY PARK

EVENTS @ TD GARDEN

200

METERS (MAXIMUM DISTANCE FROM MBTA)

6.5 MILLION VISITORS PER YEAR @ TD GARDEN + FENWAY PARK

Boston is rich with history, bursting with natural beauty and abundant in culture.
But when one of the local teams is in-season — and when is at least
one of them not? — the city is known as one thing: **the ultimate sports town.**

THE
CITY
OF
CHAMPIONS

By **PAUL FLANNERY**

* FROM AMERICAN WAY MAGAZINE DECEMBER 2011

TAKEN FROM AN AMERICAN AIRLINES FLIGHT DEPARTING FROM MIAMI

FENWAY PARK

37,493
MAXIMUM CAPACITY

3,000,000
TOTAL NUMBER OF VISITORS PER YEAR

81
NUMBER OF GAMES IN REGULAR SEASON

1912
BUILT YEAR

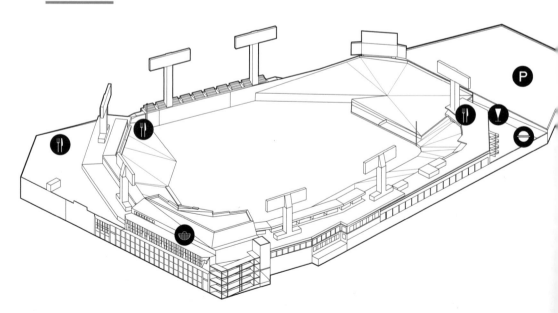

8TH
THE MOST NUMBER OF BASEBALL GAME ATTENDANCE

2ND

HIGHEST OCCUPANCY PERCENTAGE

NO CITY IN THE SUPER BOWL ERA, WHICH BEGAN IN 1967, CAN LAY CLAIM TO CHAMPIONSHIPS IN ALL FOUR MAJOR U.S. PROFESSIONAL SPORTS WITHIN A SPAN OF ONLY SIX YEARS, OR ANYTHING CLOSE. BUT WITH A STRETCH DATING TO THE PATRIOTS' NFL TITLE IN 2005, FOLLOWED BY THOSE EARNED BY THE RED SOX IN 2007 AND THE CELTICS IN 2008, BOSTON HAS JUST EARNED THE RIGHT TO SUCH A CLAIM.

* BOSTON BUSINESS JOURNAL

YEAR	GAME AVERAGE	SEASON TOTAL	A.L. AVERAGE	YEAR	GAME AVERAGE	SEASON TOTAL	A.L. AVERAGE
1912	7,754	597,096	407,954	1961	10,437	850,589	1,016,302
1913	5,791	437,194	440,851	1962	9,164	733,080	1,001,506
1914	6,055	481,359	343,449	1963	11,710	942,642	909,485
1915	6,966	539,885	304,336	1964	10,905	883,276	923,515
1916	6,364	496,397	431,486	1965	8,052	652,201	886,076
1917	4,941	387,856	357,357	1966	10,014	811,172	1,016,674
1918	3,961	249,513	213,500	1967	21,331	1,727,832	1,133,692
1919	6,048	417,291	456,780	1968	23,960	1,940,788	1,131,739
1920	5,227	402,445	635,538	1969	22,633	1,833,246	1,011,227
1921	3,627	279,273	577,541	1970	19,695	1,595,278	1,007,095
1922	3,366	259,184	609,294	1971	20,725	1,678,732	989,047
1923	2,983	229,688	575,324	1972	18,603	1,441,718	953,211
1924	5,714	448,556	656,930	1973	18,284	1,481,002	1,119,467
1925	3,523	267,782	648,356	1974	19,215	1,556,411	1,087,275
1926	3,703	285,155	614,073	1975	21,857	1,748,587	1,099,119
1927	3,965	305,275	576,619	1976	23,406	1,895,846	1,221,484
1928	5,155	396,920	527,649	1977	25,771	2,074,549	1,402,825
1929	5,092	394,620	582,809	1978	28,474	2,320,643	1,466,426
1930	5,767	444,045	585,716	1979	29,414	2,353,114	1,597,999
1931	4,588	350,975	485,412	1980	24,451	1,956,092	1,563,575
1932	2,366	182,150	391,654	1981	19,637	1,060,379	1,004,713
1933	3,607	268,715	365,776	1982	24,076	1,950,124	1,648,604
1934	7,982	610,640	470,451	1983	22,004	1,782,285	1,713,647
1935	7,254	558,568	461,001	1984	20,514	1,661,618	1,711,531
1936	8,089	626,895	522,365	1985	21,922	1,786,633	1,752,302
1937	7,268	559,659	591,979	1986	26,679	2,147,641	1,798,052
1938	8,619	646,459	555,711	1987	27,550	2,231,551	1,948,382
1939	7,540	573,070	533,825	1988	30,430	2,464,851	2,035,688
1940	9,302	716,234	679,224	1989	30,988	2,510,012	2,132,090
1941	9,271	718,497	613,995	1990	31,222	2,528,986	2,166,590
1942	9,610	730,340	525027	1991	31,635	2,562,435	2,294,113
1943	4,623	358,275	462,071	1992	30,476	2,468,574	2,268,524
1944	6,500	506,975	599,770	1993	29,901	2,422,021	2,380,955
1945	7,692	603,794	697,553	1994	30,884	1,775,818	1,728,728
1946	18,166	1,416,944	1,202,648	1995	30,061	2,164,410	1,811,356
1947	18,182	1,427,315	1,185,759	1996	28,583	2,315,231	2,122,721
1948	20,114	1,558,798	1,393,762	1997	27,483	2,226,136	2,234,523
1949	20,602	1,596,650	1,341,331	1998	28,577	2,314,704	2,298,169
1950	17,456	1,344,080	1,142,795	1999	30,201	2,446,162	2,286,874
1951	17,043	1,312,282	1,110,334	2000	31,925	2,585,895	2,262,557
1952	14,490	1,115,750	1,036,737	2001	32,412	2,625,333	2,346,071
1953	13,414	1,026,133	870,510	2002	32,717	2,650,063	2,207,891
1954	11,938	931,127	990,296	2003	33,631	2,724,165	2,191,745
1955	15,626	1,203,200	1,117,871	2004	35,028	2,837,304	2,340,422
1956	14,673	1,137,158	986,710	2005	35,166	2,813,354	2,360,452
1957	15,339	1,181,087	1,024,527	2006	36,182	2,930,768	2,458,741
1958	13,897	1,077,047	912,004	2007	36,675	2,970,755	2,527,968
1959	12,781	984,102	1,143,682	2008	37,632	3,048,250	2,464,986
1960	14,674	1,129,866	1,153,316	2009	37,811	3,062,699	2,305,178

THEN MASSACHUSETTS BAY TRANSIT AUTHORITY (MBTA) PROVIDES NUMEROUS CONVENIENT WAYS FOR RED SOX FANS TO GET TO FENWAY PARK USING PUBLIC TRANSPORTATION. THE RED SOX STRONGLY ENCOURAGE ALL FANS TO TAKE PUBLIC TRANSPORTATION TO THE GAME.

BOSTON

LOS ANGELES

CHICAGO

PHILADELPHIA

SURFACE PARKING NEAR STADIUM

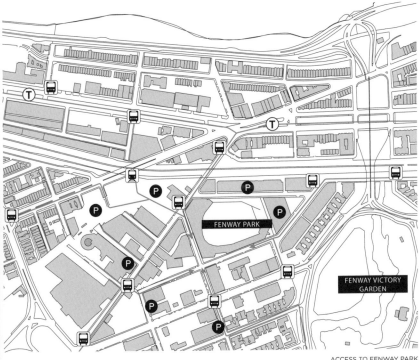

FENWAY PARK

FENWAY VICTORY GARDEN

ACCESS TO FENWAY PARK

208
209

TD GARDEN

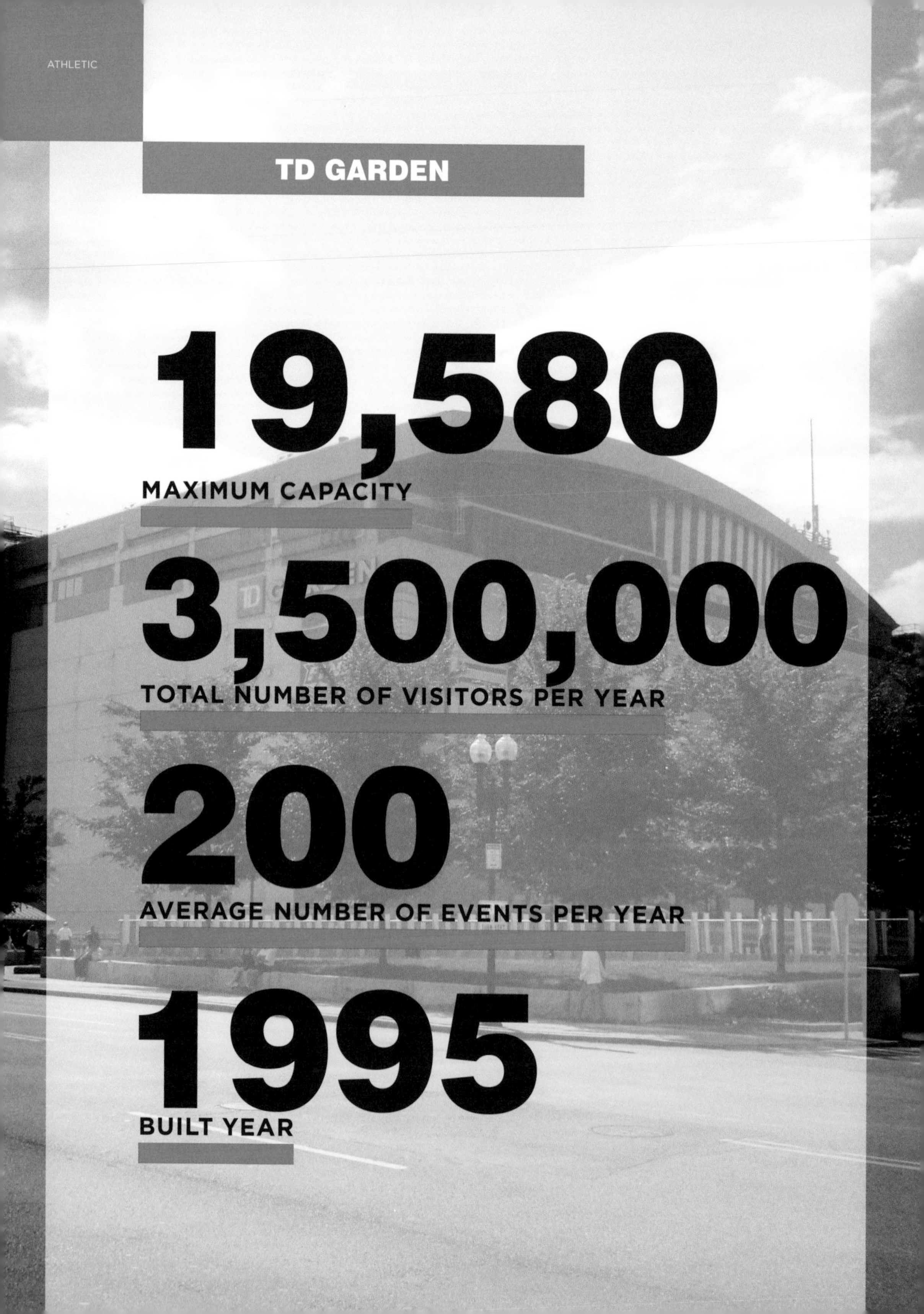

19,580

MAXIMUM CAPACITY

3,500,000

TOTAL NUMBER OF VISITORS PER YEAR

200

AVERAGE NUMBER OF EVENTS PER YEAR

1995

BUILT YEAR

BOSTON   LOS ANGELES

CHICAGO   PHILADELPHIA

SURFACE PARKINGS NEAR STADIUM

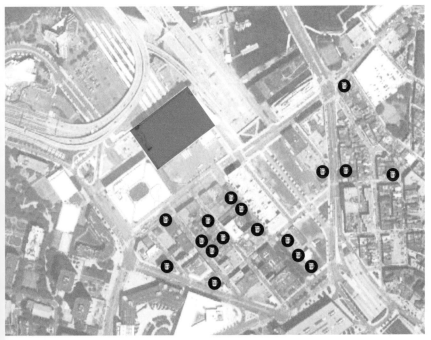

PUBS NEAR TD GARDEN

ATHLETIC CORES IN BOSTON IMPACT TO THE CITY IN VARIOUS WAYS BECAUSE THEY ARE LOCATED IN THE HEART OF THE CITY AND, MOSTLY, HAVE TO BE ACCESSED BY PUBLIC TRANSPORTATION SYSTEMS.

20%
OUTSIDE THE BOSTON METROPOLIAN AREA

8.4:1
PIZZA SOLD ON GAME DAY : NON-GAME DAY

$1.85M
ESTIMATED ECONOMIC ACTIVITY PER GAME

18,624
AVERAGE ATTENDANCE PER GAME OF CELTICS

$5M
ESTIMATED SALES DURING STANLEY CUB

TEMPOR

CORES

ARY

HYNES CONVENTION CENTER

BOSTON CONVENTION CENTER

" BOSTON IS WELL KNOWN FOR PROFESSIONAL CONFERENCES. LOCAL ECONOMY AND BUSINESSES ARE INFLUENCED BY THESE EVENTS HELD IN CONVENTIONS CENTERS.

550

MILLION
ANNUAL ECONOMIC IMPACT IN $

31.5 MILLION

= TOTAL TAX BENEFIT IN

MINUTES
TO
AIRPORT

550,000

(TOTAL NUMBER OF HOTEL ROOMS IN DEMAND)

550,00

ANNUAL ECONOMIC IMPACT IN DOLLARS

31,500,

TOTAL TAX BENEFIT IN DOLLARS

550,00

TOTAL NUMBER OF HOTEL ROOMS IN DEMAND

Two major convention centers in Boston have the best access from the Logan International Airport by both vehicle and public transportation means. It is not only because the airport is relatively close to the city but also those convention centers are located IN the city, instead of outskirts as many other cities. It means that impacts by these convention centers to the city are much stronger in many ways than any other cities that have segregated convention centers.

MAJOR CONVENTION CENTERS IN U.S

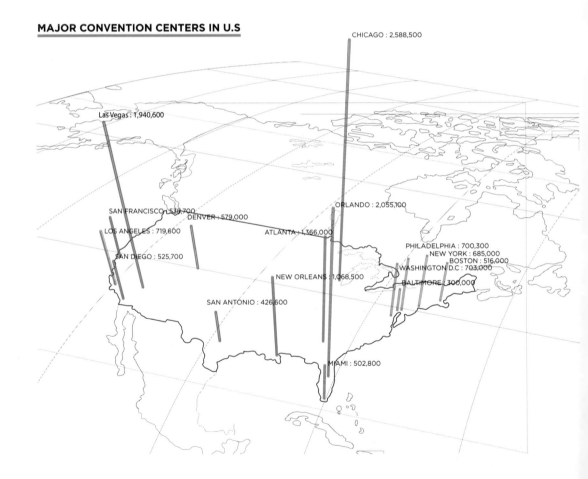

CHICAGO : 2,588,500

Las Vegas : 1,940,600

ORLANDO : 2,055,100

SAN FRANCISCO : 539,700
DENVER : 579,000
LOS ANGELES : 719,600
ATLANTA : 1,366,000

SAN DIEGO : 525,700

PHILADELPHIA : 700,300
NEW YORK : 685,000
BOSTON : 516,000
WASHINGTON D.C : 703,000
BALTIMORE : 300,000

NEW ORLEANS : 1,068,500

SAN ANTONIO : 426,600

MIAMI : 502,800

ANNUAL ECONOMIC IMPACT BY SECTOR

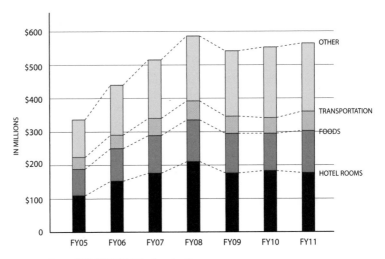

Source : MCCA; IMPLAN Model for Massachusetts

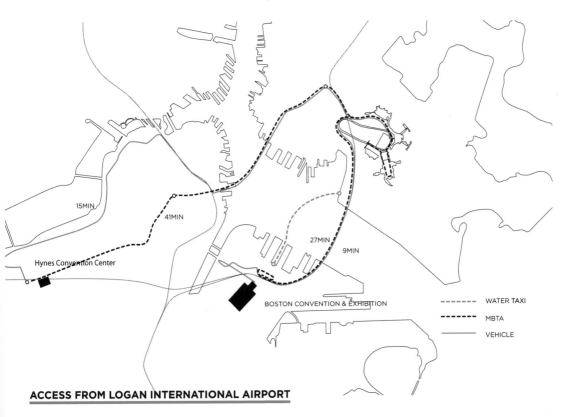

ACCESS FROM LOGAN INTERNATIONAL AIRPORT

BOSTON CONVENTION CENTER

NUMBERS SINCE BCEC

213,676
TOTAL SQUARE METER OF OFFICE SPACE

750
TOTAL NUMBER OF NEW APARTMENTS

40
TOTAL NUMBER OF NEW RESTAURANTS

4.7
TOTAL ACRE OF PARKS

1,900
TOTAL NUMBER OF NEW WORKERS

1,671
TOTAL NUMBER OF HOTEL ROOMS

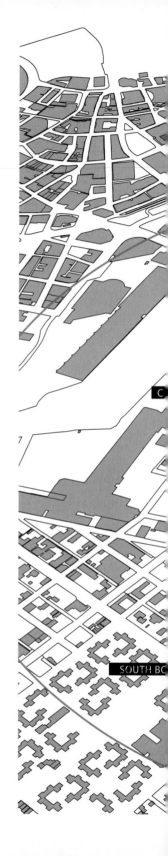

SOUTH BC

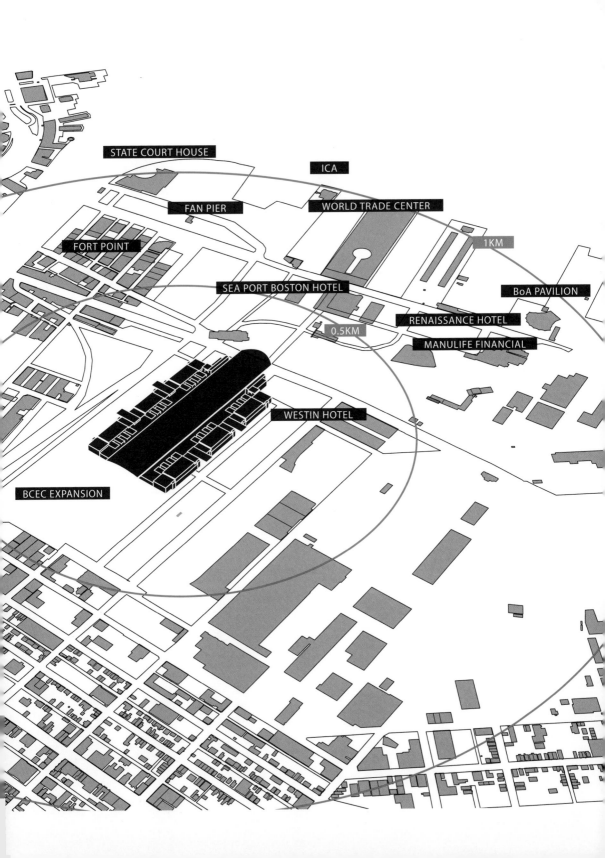

STATE COURT HOUSE

ICA

FAN PIER

WORLD TRADE CENTER

FORT POINT

1KM

SEA PORT BOSTON HOTEL

BoA PAVILION

RENAISSANCE HOTEL

0.5KM

MANULIFE FINANCIAL

WESTIN HOTEL

BCEC EXPANSION

SCALE COMPARISON

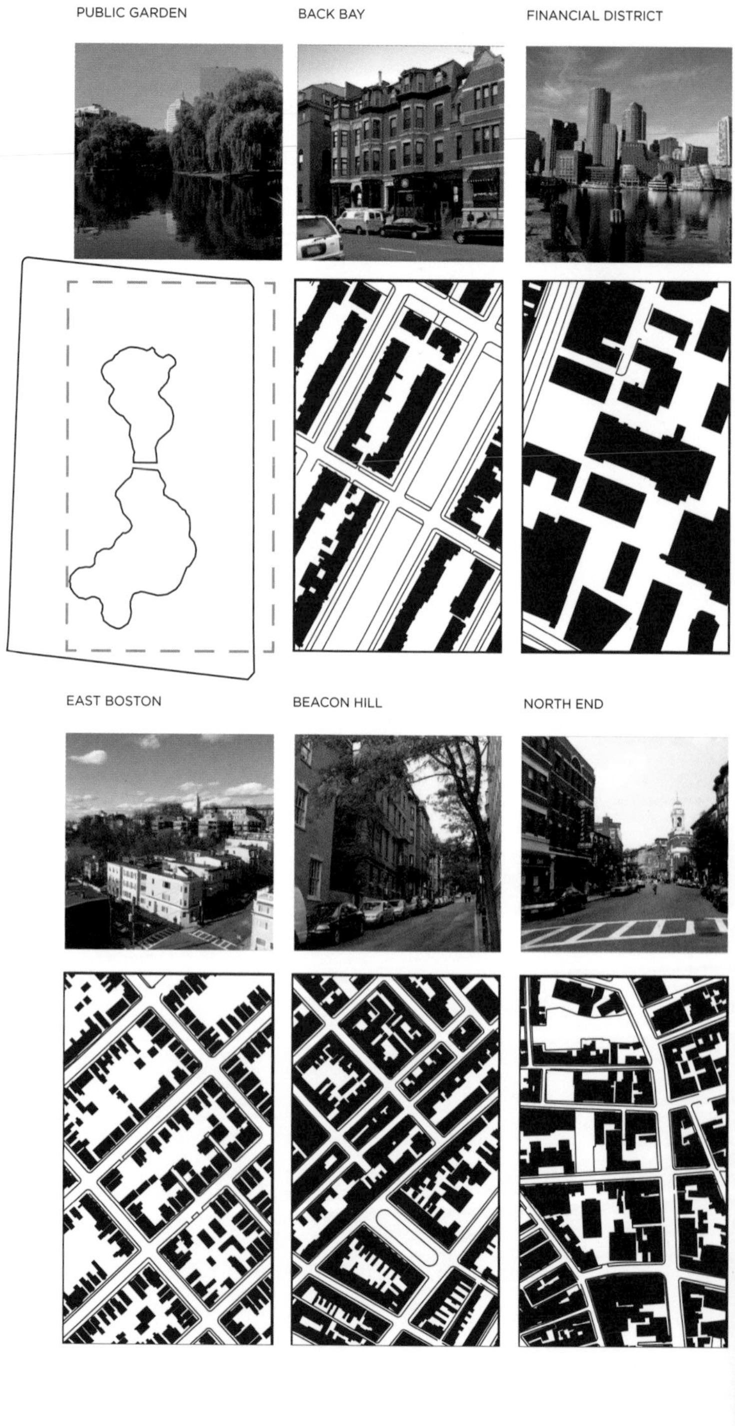

PUBLIC GARDEN

BACK BAY

FINANCIAL DISTRICT

EAST BOSTON

BEACON HILL

NORTH END

47,937
TOTAL EXHIBITION AREA

14,864
TOTAL MEETING AREA

3,716
TOTAL BALLROOM AREA

27,870
TOTAL FUNCTIONAL AREA

BCEC

89,910M2
FOOT PRINT AREA

BOSTON HYNES CONVENTION CENTER

17,930

TOTAL EXHIBITION AREA

6,596

TOTAL MEETING AREA

2,229

TOTAL BALLROOM AREA

One of the most important supporting facilities for convention center is Hotel. And thus, numbers of hotels emerged in Back Bay area near the Hynes Convention Center. And thanks to the attractions of the area, new interaction starts to happen between the attendees of convenient center and the local businesses.

HOTELS NEAR HYNES CONVENTION CENTER

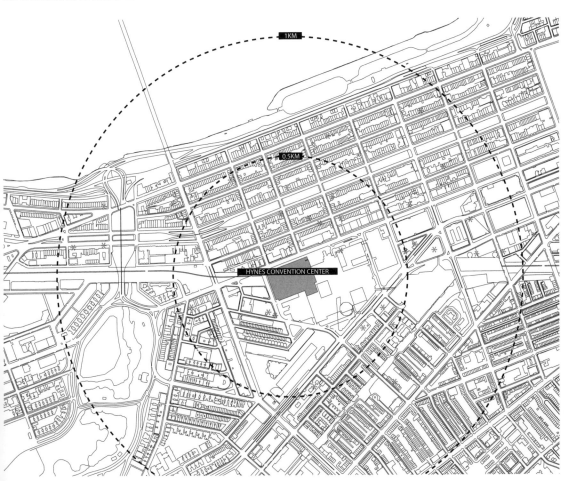

14,864 / 4,000
TOTAL FUNCTIONAL SPACE AREA / **MULTI PURPOSE AUDITORIUM CAPACITY**

BCEC AND HYNES CONVENTION CENTER WILL PLAY A MAJOR ROLE IN CATALYZING THE DEVELOPMENT OF THE INNOVATION DISTRICT. IT WILL NOT ONLY GENERATE ECONOMICAL IMPACT TO THE AREA BUT ALSO INFLUENCE PROGRAMS AND USE OF NEW DEVELOPMENTS.

We have classified buildings found in Boston that follow METROPOLITAN HYBRID qualities in order to understand Boston's current condition. Some are a continuity of the city grid in order to create a continuous urbanity, others are hybridizing infrastructure with building stock to maximize use. Even though not all of them are HYBRIDS, all of them are METROPOLITAN.

METRO-POLITAN HYBRIDS

ON HYBRIDITY

BY: RAFAEL LUNA

The concept of the hybrid building has existed throughout history, always closely linked to density and land value. Walled cities demarcated the boundary between a civilized territory and the wild. Limitations in early transportation of goods and services within the walls caused work related programs to be closely knit to residences, exemplified by the home above the shop. Stacking was a common outcome generated by the physical confinements of the city. As a result, a symbiotic relationship between living and working within the same building occurred.

At the turn of the 20th century, new economic models, led by the growth of industry inside the city, generated a growing population and an emergent social working class. The city's growth was now in direct relation to the growth of industry. The relationship of industry to the city rivaled architecture as the primary generator of urban fabric, and as industry became rationalized so did architecture. With the influence of Fordism shaping corporate architecture, the skyscraper became an icon of corporations during modernism. The Seagram Building by Mies Van Der Rohe in New York helped define the skyscraper as the corporate vehicle; a reflection of density and monoculture in the metropolis. But the invention of the skyscraper meant a lot more. The skyscraper substitutes any bi-dimensional urban planning into vertical components of the city grid, which incorporates elements of the public realm into a private sector, making the skyscraper a component of organization for the city. This meant that the skyscraper allowed for a mixing of public and private programming reflecting the nature of the city within itself; a city within a city, and with this the birth of the metropolitan hybrid.

In 1985, Joseph Fenton assembled a catalog of hybrid buildings for Pamphlet Architecture, and established them as models for revitalizing American Cities. These hybrid buildings were in large part produced as a consequence of the constraints of the urban grid in a growing Metropolis. Although all of the hybrid buildings are multi-programmed, they differ from mixed-use buildings. Hybrid buildings generate a complex relationship between program, technology, urban context and society. By Fenton's definition, a hybrid building also differentiates itself from mega-structures by delimiting itself to the city grid that promotes verticality due to escalating land value and horizontal restrictions. Hybrid buildings were largely developed in America from the end of the 19th century until 1929, when the Great Depression

MIXED-USE BUILDINGS ARE PROGRAMED WITH DIVERSE FUNCTIONS FROM THE BEGINNING; THEY HAVE DESIGNATED SPACES FOR DESIGNATED FUNCTIONS. HYBRID BUILDINGS, ARE ALWAYS CHANGING OR ADAPTING TO THE CITY IN TRUE METROPOLITAN FASHION

"

slowed all new construction plans. Shortly after, the Modernist conference, CIAM IV, promoted segregation of land use, supported by the Charter of Athens, which categorized new buildings by single use. Hybrid buildings did not regain footing until after World War II, when renewed interest in zoning laws and the re-invigoration of American urban cores was revived.

Fenton suggested that hybrid buildings generate two categories of pro-gramming: thematic and disparate. The thematic building generates a dependency between its parts and an interaction of elements. The disparate building, on the other hand, has a schizophrenic, fragmented relationship of parts, where pieces coexist in a mutual alliance. Thematic hybrids suggest a singleness where program-matic elements form a functional ensemble. Disparate hybrids promote an economic advantage because of their diversified programing.

The hybrid buildings cataloged by Fenton are also categorized into three groups based on form: Fabric, Graft, and Monolith. Fabric hybrids suppress their program under a single envelope that generates an inconspicuous overall appear-ance. It adheres to site conditions in order to generate urban fabric. Graft hybrids express their program on the exterior in an apparent union between building types. Monolith hybrids generally represent a section of the city within its monumental scale, accommodating the greatest diversity of functions and versatility in the city.

Opposed to Fenton's argument, American architect Steven Holl suggests that hybrid buildings are not caused by the pressures of density and the metropolitan condition, but as a response to the dispersion and frequency of deformed towns. Free standing corporate headquarters, industrial parks, shopping centers, malls, and suburban housing scattered through the countryside have dissipated town centers that strongly need revitalization. Hybrid buildings are physical architectural forms that concentrate activity to invigorate urban life. The hybrid building is manifested as an individual form that supports the underlying pattern of the city grid in order to clarify edge conditions for the city; what is urban versus rural or countryside. In this argument, a hybrid building should be understood in terms of its programmatic diversity that reinstates components of city life in order to invigorate the city or create a new urban core.

Fenton's and Holl's arguments apply directly to American and European cities where density is lower than Asian cites and their evolution is more gradual. Tokyo, for example, has evolved differently from European cities in the sense that their building stock is replaced every 30 to 40 years using the contemporary technology of the time. European cities have a culture of recycling building stock, which impedes their ability to generate a variety of spatial or functional configurations that are only possible with new building technology. "No-good" architecture, as named by Atelier Bow-Wow, has formed the urban fabric of Tokyo by creating coherent environments within the city. These buildings are defined as hybrids where unrelated functions coexist under a single structure; there is a joint utilization of several different and adjacent buildings and structures, and they condense unusual urban ecology in a single building. Some of these buildings can be cross-categorized between architecture, urban, civil, and landscape. Infrastructure like highways, train stations, and ventilation ducts, perform a greater cultural role than mere infrastructure. Raised expressways are in some cases in-filled with extra program like retail, offices, and housing. The pressures of land value and density has forced additional program into any empty void and urban gap. There is an urban connectivity between the systems of transportation and buildings, so that the city works in a continuous metropolitan flow. In 2001, Atelier Bow-Wow produced a catalog, similar to Fenton's catalog of American hybrids, where they classify "No-good architecture" in Tokyo. By cataloging all these "no-good" buildings, Atelier Bow Wow showed the relevance of studying these scenarios as hybrid resultants of Tokyo's density. These are buildings that have not been designed by famous architects, nor have uniqueness to their form or architectural aesthetic. Yet, their programmatic combinations speak of the possibility of non-related functions to symbiotically coexist within a single building. More importantly, it marks a clear distinction between a "mixed-use" building versus a hybrid building. Mixed-use buildings are programed with diverse functions from the beginning; they have designated spaces for designated functions. Hybrid buildings, are always changing or adapting to the city in true metropolitan fashion. Just as

Fenton suggested that hybrids represent a barometer that records the evolution of society, Tokyo's "No-good" architecture are a concrete report of Tokyo's Metropolitan condition.

Unlike Tokyo's hybrids repertoire, housing stock composes the majority of city fabric in most cities. As density increases, the housing supply becomes a major issue for the expansion of the city. The early 20th century Modernists, Bruno Taut and Walter Gropius, explored the minimum dwelling as a family condenser that hybridized functions within the same household. Kitchen and bathroom could be united as a wet room. The family living room was also used as the bedroom for the children with the rational that living rooms are only in use when the parents are awake. Once the head of the family goes to sleep , so does the rest of the family and the living room no longer has a purpose. Hybridity occurred by an optimization of function by time. A single space can be used for different functions based on the time of occupancy. Current demographics demand for a different type of housing stock though. In fast growing cities, there is a continuous flow of a floating population of immigrants and commuters. Housing demands an increasing flexibility. In "Specific Neutrality, A manifesto for new collective housing", Atelier Kempe Thill argue for flexibility from the housing unit, developer, and construction methods. They suggest that future housing stock should have a certain neutrality of use that allows for the flexibility and adaptability of the building. By constructing these neutral settings, new hybrid possibilities are created where housing stock could also function as offices, retail, and so forth, promoting a metropolitan condition within the building.

This neutral settings can be interpreted as autonomy in architecture; an architectural language stripped of historical traits or programmatic associations, somewhat as an empty stage for metropolitan events. Bernard Tschumi, an architect most closely associated with Deconstructivism, explores the autonomy of architecture in Parc de la Villette as a setting for hybridity. Schizophrenic places, and objects on the same plane without distinguishable origins generate a hybrid sense of place with no specific typological connotation. A single architectural form no longer implies a single function but a setting for diverse variations. He achieves this architecturally by modes of cross-programming, where typologies are displaced, and trans-programming, where programs can be combined. Combinations and permutations amongst different categories of analysis, not composition or expression of function, generate new programmatic relations creating event spaces for hybridity.

In conclusion, there is a direct correlation between hybrid buildings and a metropolitan condition. Fenton suggests that they appear as result of escalating land values, and density. Holl argues that they are means of revitalizing cities that lack urban cores. They also appear as resultants from optimization of land use. The hybrid condition occurs not by directly juxtaposing the layouts for different programs, but by allowing the building to serve as a more neutral setting for events. This neutrality allows for endless arrangements of functions to occur within the same building while providing building stock for the city to grow dynamically and flexibly.

The hybrid building is a barometer recording the evolution of our society. Each new
juxtaposition reflects a willingness to con-
front the present, and to extend exploration
into the future.

Joseph Fenton

HYBRID

≠

MIXED-USE

FIRST HYBRID BUILDING IN BOSTON?

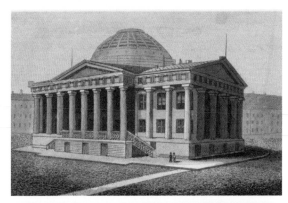

1837

1915

The United States Custom House is the result of grafting two buildings, the original domed two story Boston Custom House designed by Ammi B. Young in 1837, and a 500 foot office tower added above it by Peabody and Stearns almost on hundreds years later. Elevators, stairs and corner structural piers penetrate the rotunda at its perimeter, leaving the dome intact.

The decision to graft an office tower onto the original Custom House was attributed to escalating land values of the centrally located site occupied by a historically significant building. In this example of an 'over-building', the hybrid solution illustrates its capacity to rejuvenate existing structures within the city fabric.

Joseph Fenton, Pamphlet Architecture No.11

UNITED STATES CUSTOM HOUSE

ADDRESS: 3 MCKINLEY SQUARE, BOSTON, MA

YEAR: 1837

PROGRAM: CUSTOM HOUSE
OFFICE
HOTEL (SINCE 1997)

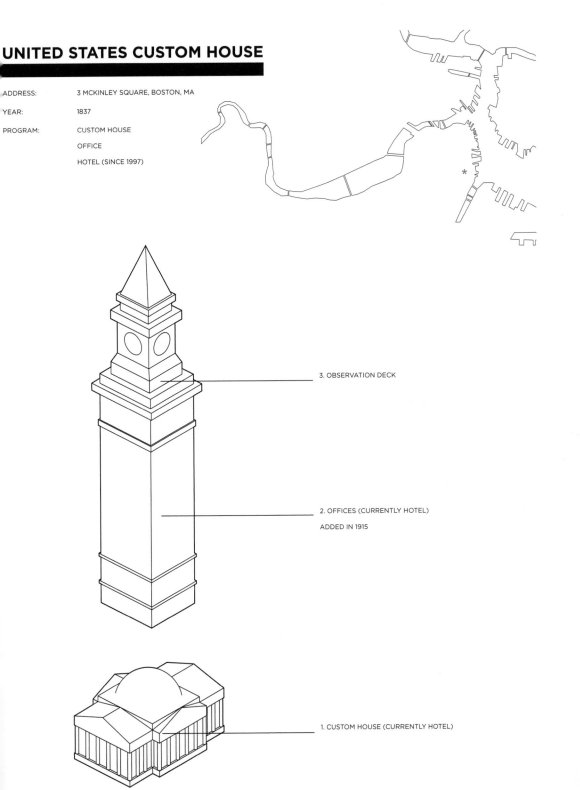

3. OBSERVATION DECK

2. OFFICES (CURRENTLY HOTEL)
ADDED IN 1915

1. CUSTOM HOUSE (CURRENTLY HOTEL)

BOSTON HYBRIDS

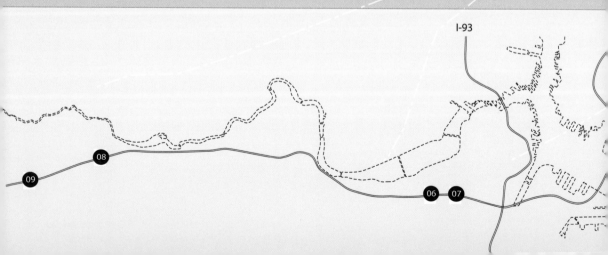

GOVERNMENT CENTER PARKING

ADDRESS: 50 NEW SUDBURY STREET, BOSTON, MA

YEAR:

PROGRAM:
PARKING
OFFICE
RETAIL
MBTA SUBWAY STATION
MBTA BUS STOP

MBTA BUS STOP

| 92, 93, 111, 325, 326, 424, |
| 426, 428, 434, 441, 442, |
| 450, 455 |

MBTA ORANGE / GREEN LINE

PARKING

OFFICE

RETAIL

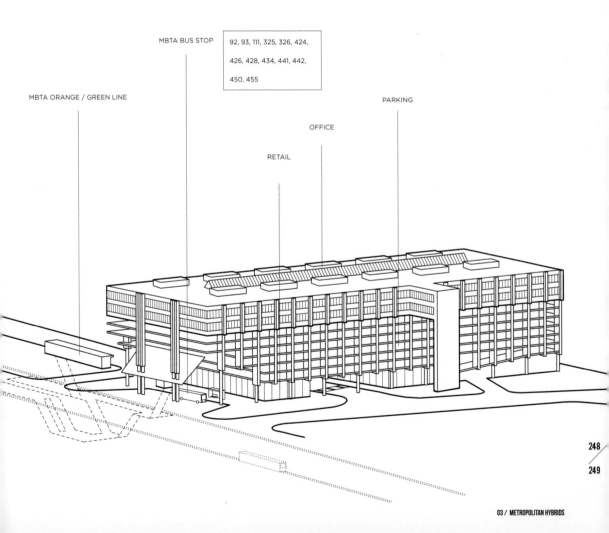

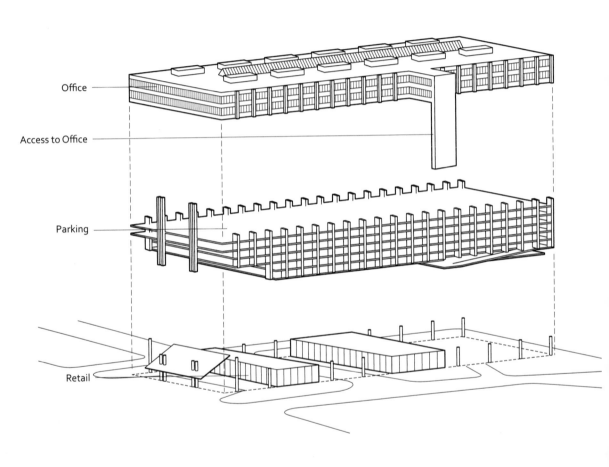

Office

Access to Office

Parking

Retail

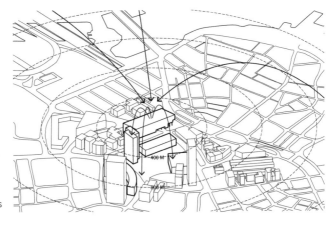

DAYTIME : PARKING FOR COMMUTERS

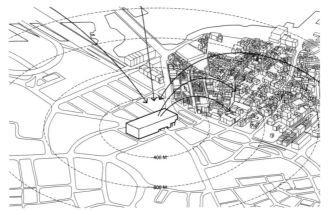

NIGHTTIME : PARKING FOR NEIGHBORHOODS

LINCOLN STREET GARAGE

ADDRESS: 125 LINCOLN STREET, BOSTON, MA

YEAR: 1999

PROGRAM: GROCERY

     PARKING

     OFFICE

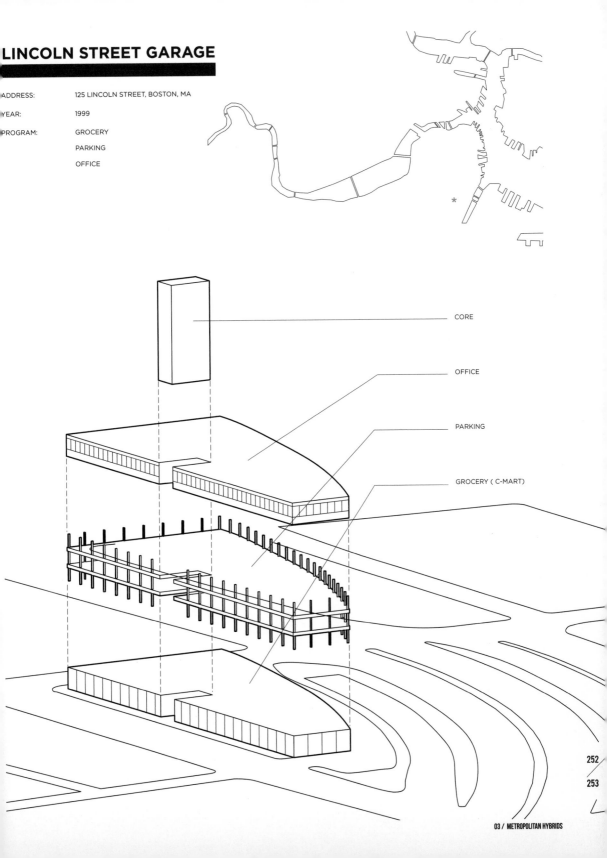

CORE

OFFICE

PARKING

GROCERY (C-MART)

252
253

MUSEUM OF SCIENCE

ADDRESS: 1 SCIENCE PARK, BOSTON, MA

YEAR: 1951

PROGRAM: MUSEUM

                PARKING

                CANAL

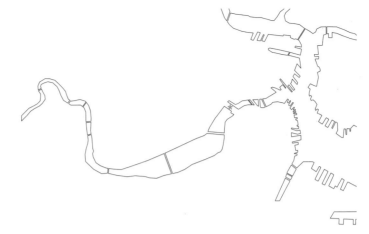

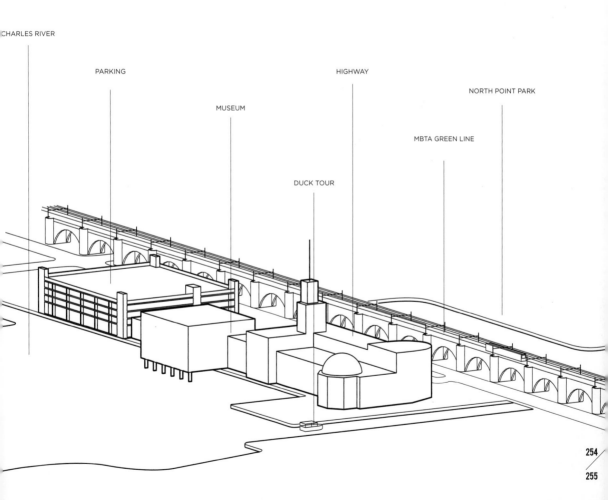

CHARLES RIVER

PARKING

MUSEUM

DUCK TOUR

HIGHWAY

NORTH POINT PARK

MBTA GREEN LINE

254
255

BUILDING FIGUREGROUND

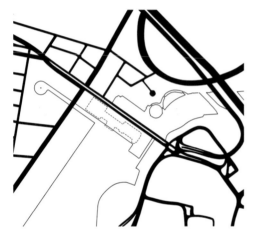

STREET FIGUREGROUND

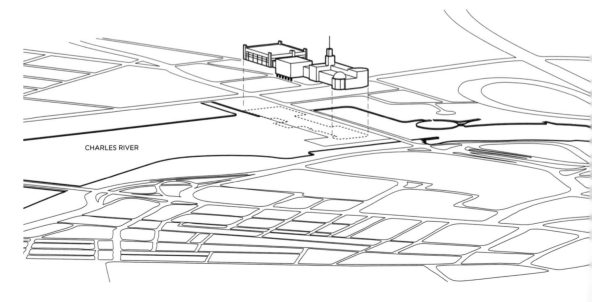

CHARLES RIVER

EXHAUST BUILDING

ADDRESS: 136 BLACKSTON STREET, BOSTON, MA

YEAR: 2009

PROGRAM: MBTA SUBWAY STATION

HIGHWAY VENTILATION

PARKING

OFFICE

RETAIL

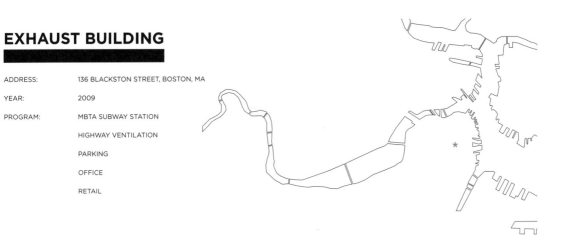

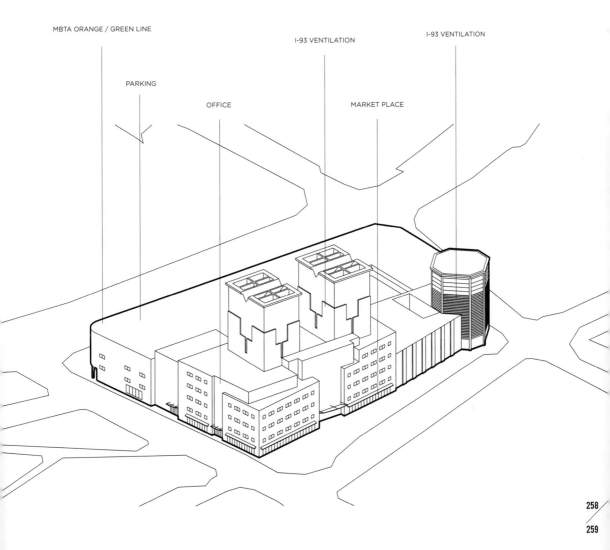

MBTA ORANGE / GREEN LINE

PARKING

OFFICE

I-93 VENTILATION

MARKET PLACE

I-93 VENTILATION

258 / 259

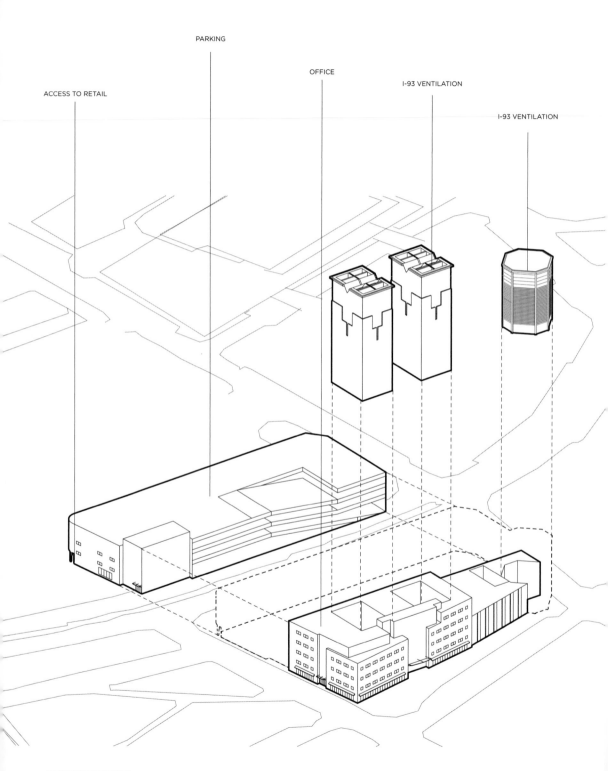

ACCESS TO RETAIL

PARKING

OFFICE

I-93 VENTILATION

I-93 VENTILATION

I WANT TO BE METROPOLITAN

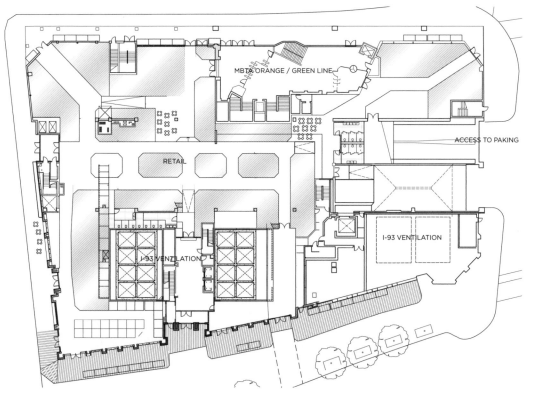

MBTA ORANGE / GREEN LINE

ACCESS TO PAKING

RETAIL

I-93 VENTILATION

I-93 VENTILATION

PRUDENTIAL CENTER

ADDRESS: 800 BOYLSTON, BOSTON, MA

YEAR: 1964

PROGRAM: MBTA SUBWAY STATION
            I-90 HIGHWAY
            CONVENTION CENTER
            HOTEL
            RESIDENCE
            OFFICE
            RETAIL
            PARKING

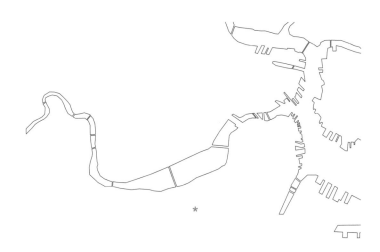

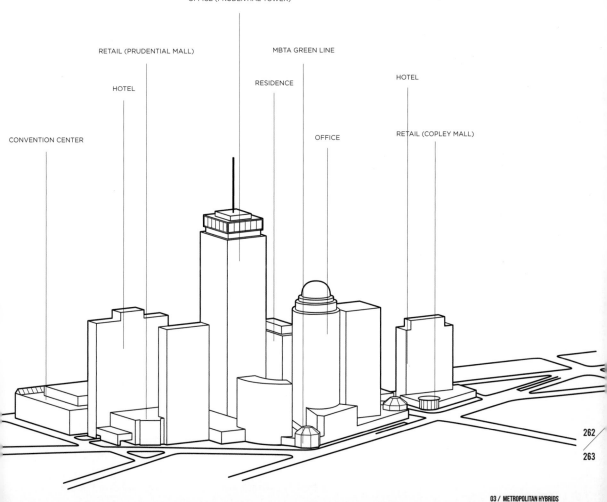

OFFICE (PRUDENTIAL TOWER)

RETAIL (PRUDENTIAL MALL)

MBTA GREEN LINE

HOTEL

RESIDENCE

HOTEL

CONVENTION CENTER

OFFICE

RETAIL (COPLEY MALL)

262
263

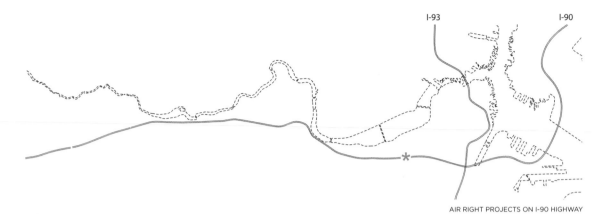

AIR RIGHT PROJECTS ON I-90 HIGHWAY

1920S

1960 PRUDENTIAL MASTER PLAN

2000S PRUDENTIAL CENTER

I WANT TO BE METROPOLITAN

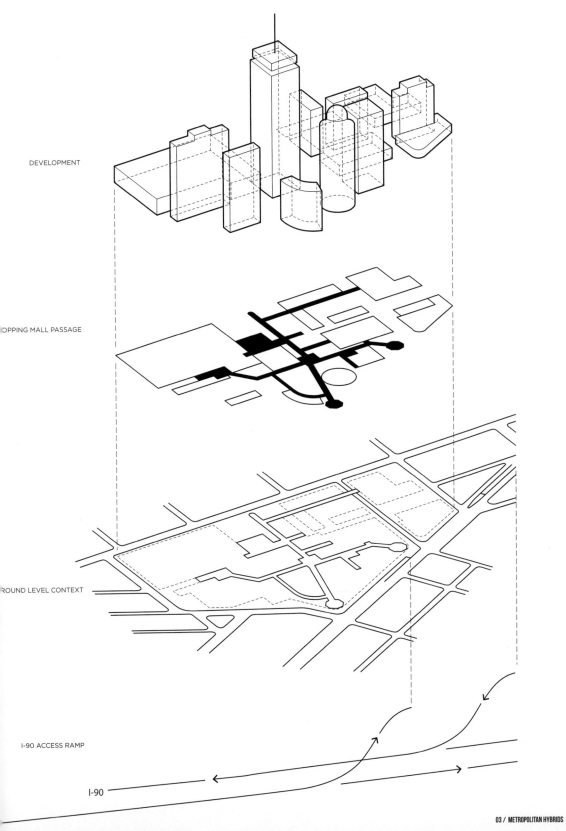

DEVELOPMENT

SHOPPING MALL PASSAGE

GROUND LEVEL CONTEXT

I-90 ACCESS RAMP

I-90

DARTMOUTH STREET GARAGE

ADDRESS: 126 DARTMOUTH STREET, BOSTON, MA

YEAR:

PROGRAM: PARKING

                I-90 HIGHWAY

                MBTA SUBWAY STATION

                MBTA COMMUTER RAIL STATION

                MBTA BUS STOP

                HIGHWAY VENTILATION TOWER

I-93

I-90

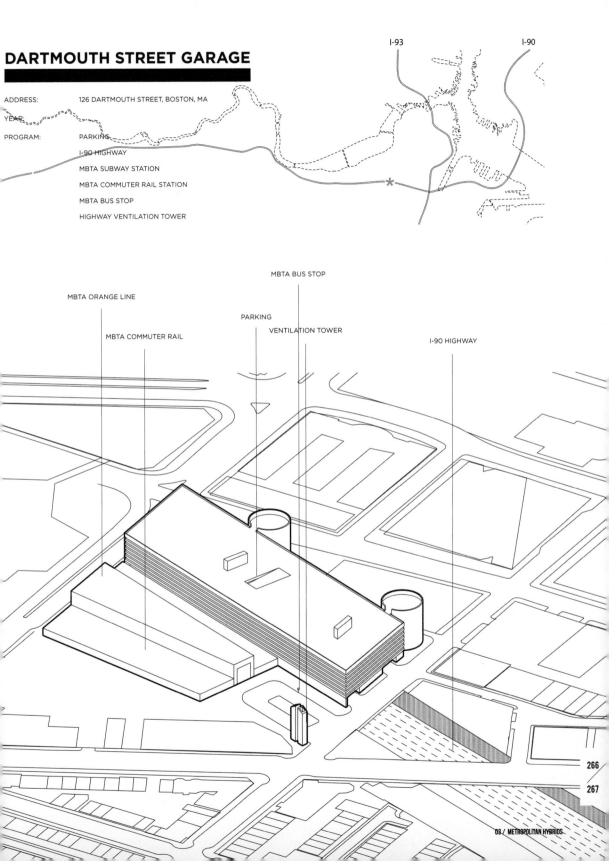

MBTA BUS STOP

MBTA ORANGE LINE

PARKING

MBTA COMMUTER RAIL

VENTILATION TOWER

I-90 HIGHWAY

266

267

03 / METROPOLITAN HYBRIDS

CROWN PLAZA HOTEL

ADDRESS: 320 WASHINGTON STREET, NEWTON, MA

YEAR:

PROGRAM: HOTEL

I-90 HIGHWAY

OFFICE

PARKING

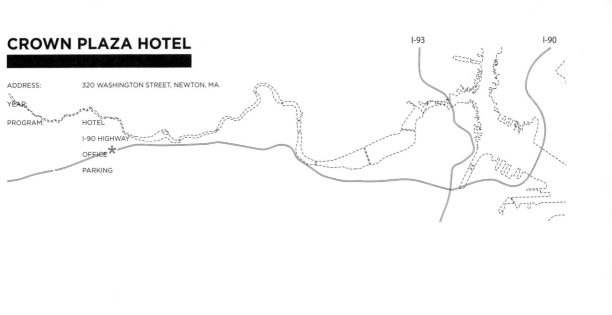

MBTA COMMUTER RAIL

PARKING

HOTEL (CROWN PLAZA)

OFFICE

I-90 HIGHWAY

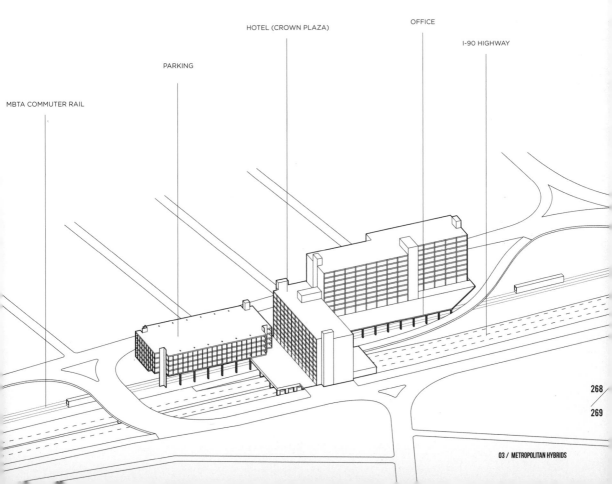

268
269

SHAWS IN NEWTONVILLE

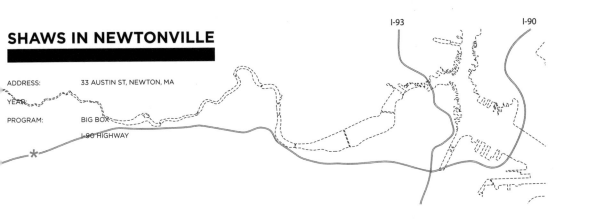

ADDRESS: 33 AUSTIN ST, NEWTON, MA

YEAR:

PROGRAM: BIG BOX

                I-90 HIGHWAY

*

I-93   I-90

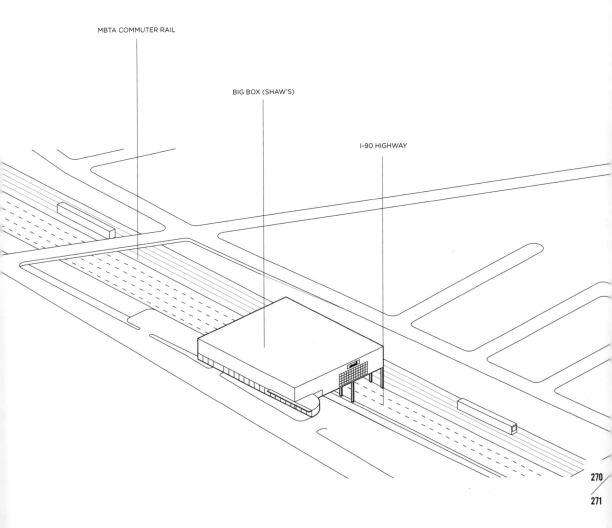

MBTA COMMUTER RAIL

BIG BOX (SHAW'S)

I-90 HIGHWAY

270

271

TUFTS MEDICAL CENTER

ADDRESS: 800 WASHINGTON STREET, BOSTON, MA

YEAR:

PROGRAM: MEDICAL FACILITIES

PARKING

MBTA SUBWAY STATION

WASHINGTON STREET

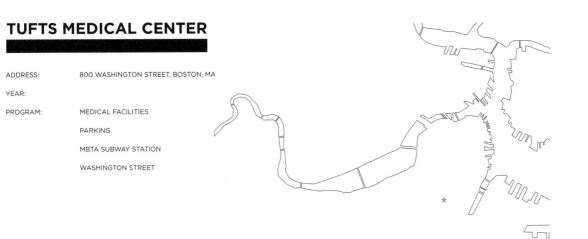

MEDICAL FACILITIES

MBTA ORANGE LINE

MBTA SILVER LINE

WASHINGTON STREET

PARKING

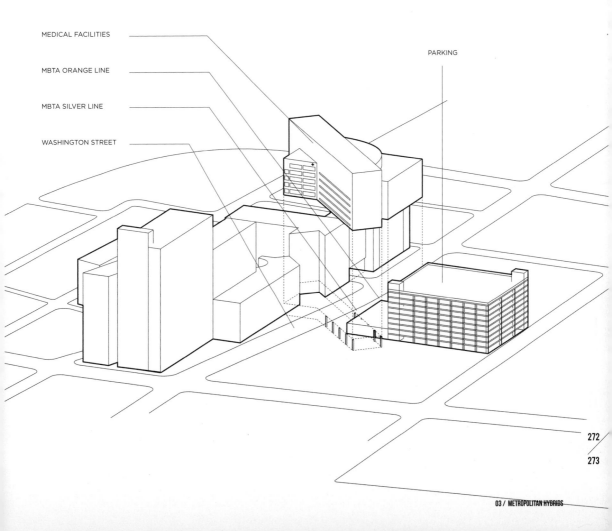

272
273

BOSTON MEDICAL CENTER

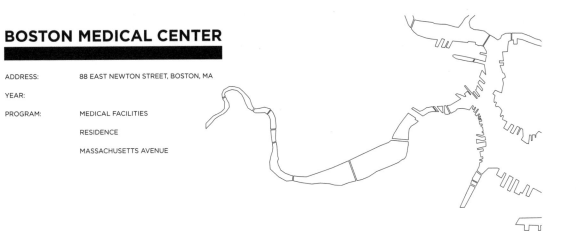

ADDRESS: 88 EAST NEWTON STREET, BOSTON, MA

YEAR:

PROGRAM: MEDICAL FACILITIES

                 RESIDENCE

                 MASSACHUSETTS AVENUE

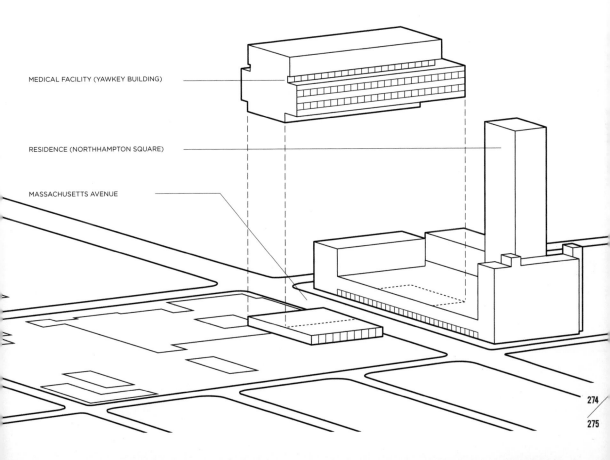

MEDICAL FACILITY (YAWKEY BUILDING)

RESIDENCE (NORTHHAMPTON SQUARE)

MASSACHUSETTS AVENUE

274
275

CambridgeSide

EW YORK COMPANY LANE RYAN

GALLERIA

CAMBRIDGE
150
492-1100

CAMBRIDGESIDE GALLERIA

ADDRESS: 100 CAMBRIDGESIDE PLACE, CAMBRIDGE MA

YEAR: 1990

PROGRAM: SHOPPING MALL

             BIG BOX

             HOTEL

             OFFICE

             PARKING

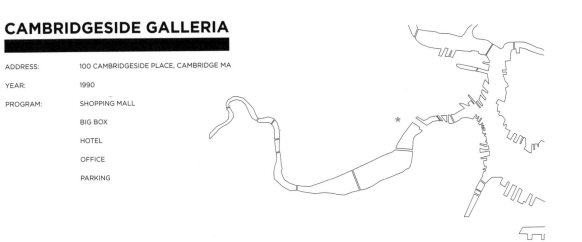

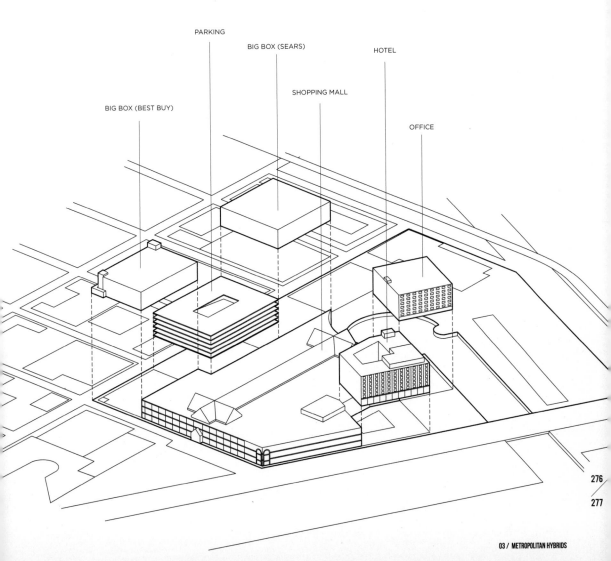

PARKING

BIG BOX (SEARS)

SHOPPING MALL

HOTEL

OFFICE

BIG BOX (BEST BUY)

BEST BUY ON NEWBURY ST.

ADDRESS: 360 NEWBURY STREET, BOSTON, MA

YEAR: 1988

PROGRAM: BIG BOX
RESIDENCE
MBTA SUBWAY

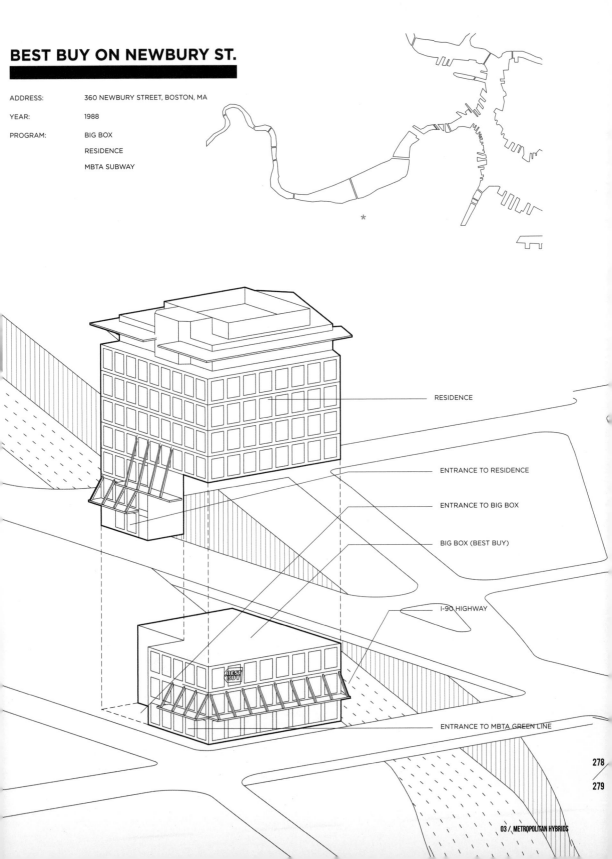

RESIDENCE

ENTRANCE TO RESIDENCE

ENTRANCE TO BIG BOX

BIG BOX (BEST BUY)

I-90 HIGHWAY

ENTRANCE TO MBTA GREEN LINE

278
279

SHAWS+ LE MERIDIEN

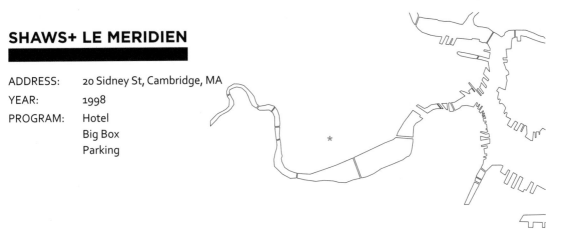

ADDRESS: 20 Sidney St, Cambridge, MA

YEAR: 1998

PROGRAM: Hotel
Big Box
Parking

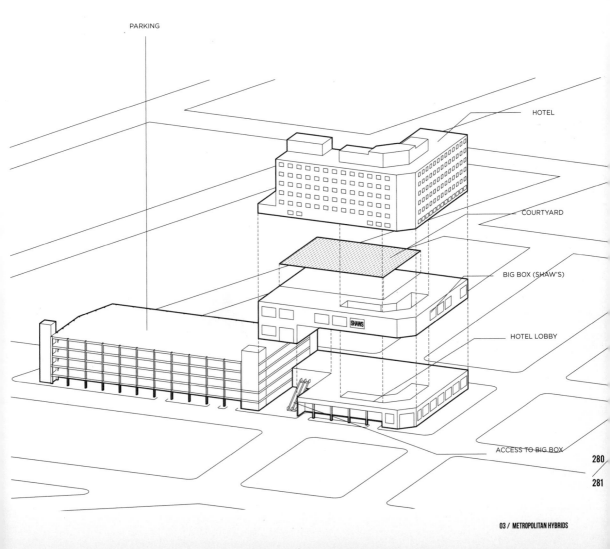

PARKING

HOTEL

COURTYARD

BIG BOX (SHAW'S)

SHAWS

HOTEL LOBBY

ACCESS TO BIG BOX

280
281

BASKETBALL CITY BOSTON

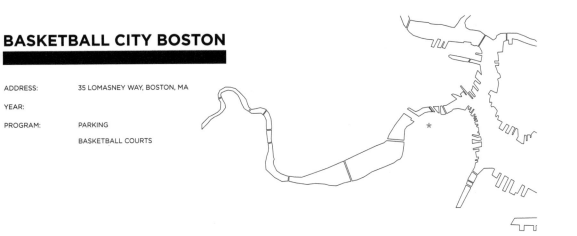

ADDRESS: 35 LOMASNEY WAY, BOSTON, MA

YEAR:

PROGRAM: PARKING

                BASKETBALL COURTS

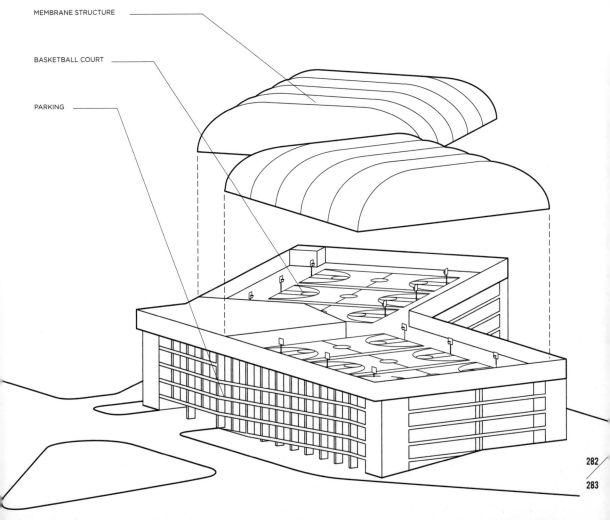

MEMBRANE STRUCTURE

BASKETBALL COURT

PARKING

MIDDLESEX COUNTY JAIL

ADDRESS: 40 THORNDIKE STREET, CAMBRIDGE, MA

YEAR: 1971

PROGRAM: COUNTY JAIL

                    COUNTY COURTHOUSE

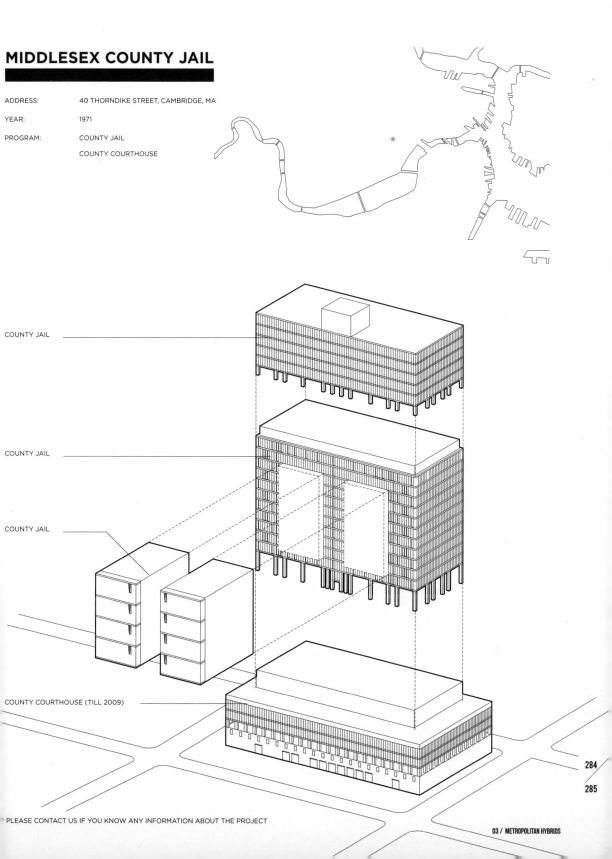

COUNTY JAIL

COUNTY JAIL

COUNTY JAIL

COUNTY COURTHOUSE (TILL 2009)

PLEASE CONTACT US IF YOU KNOW ANY INFORMATION ABOUT THE PROJECT

RUGGLES STATION

ADDRESS: 150 FORSYTH STREET, ROXBURY, MA

YEAR: 1987

PROGRAM: MBTA SUBWAY STATION

              MBTA COMMUTER RAIL STATION

              MBTA BUS STOP

              INSTITUTION

              PARKING

              RETAIL

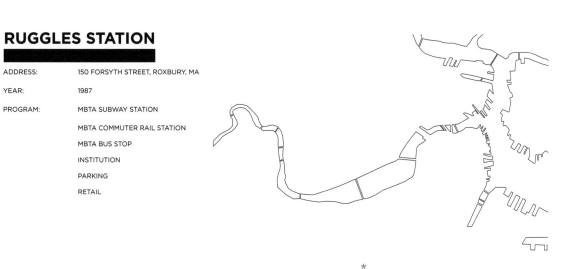

*

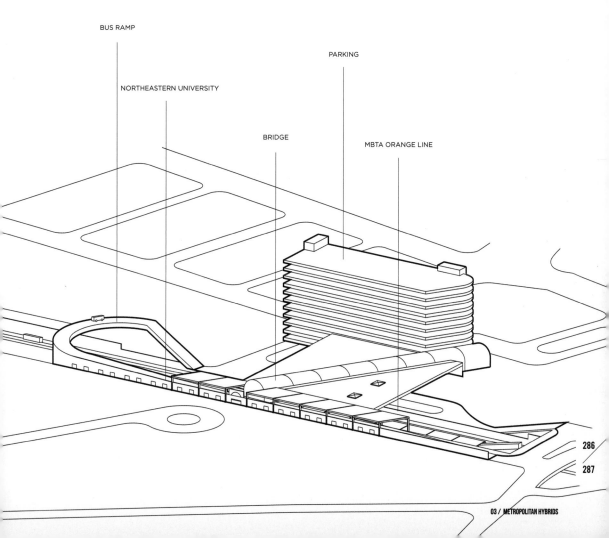

BUS RAMP

NORTHEASTERN UNIVERSITY

PARKING

BRIDGE

MBTA ORANGE LINE

286
287

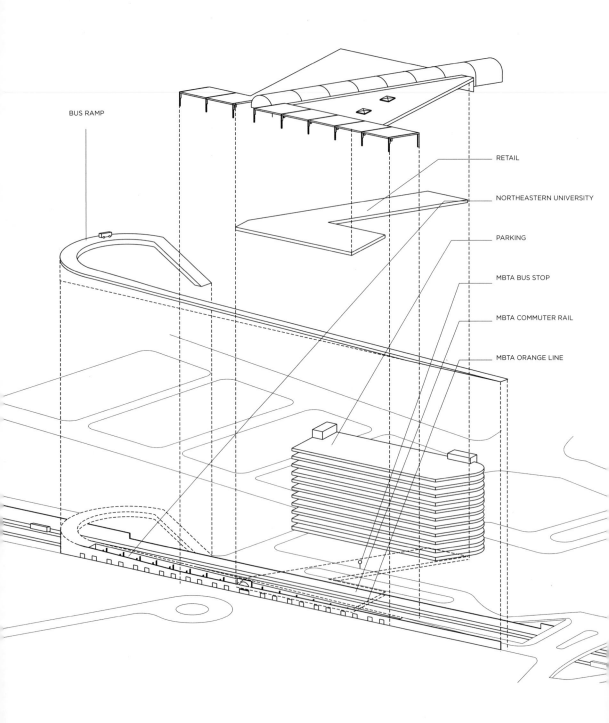

BUS RAMP

RETAIL

NORTHEASTERN UNIVERSITY

PARKING

MBTA BUS STOP

MBTA COMMUTER RAIL

MBTA ORANGE LINE

BRIDGE / PLATFORM

NORTHEASTERN UNIVERSITY

MBTA BUS STOP

SOUTH STATION + BUS TERMINAL

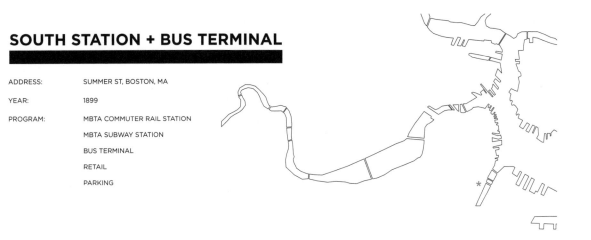

ADDRESS: SUMMER ST, BOSTON, MA

YEAR: 1899

PROGRAM: MBTA COMMUTER RAIL STATION

                MBTA SUBWAY STATION

                BUS TERMINAL

                RETAIL

                PARKING

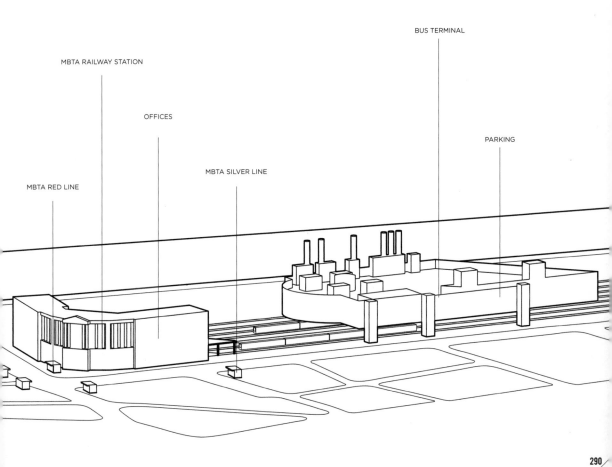

MBTA RAILWAY STATION

OFFICES

MBTA SILVER LINE

MBTA RED LINE

BUS TERMINAL

PARKING

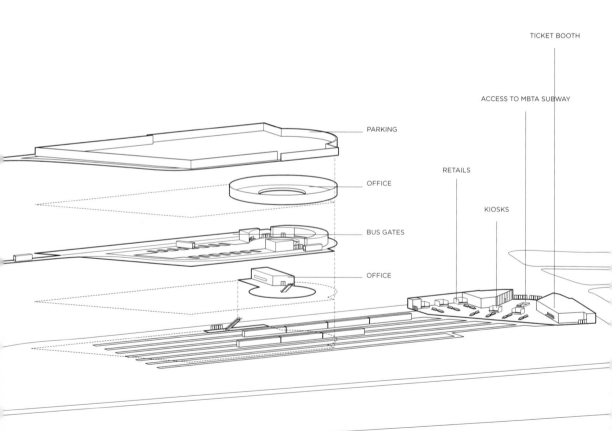

PARKING

OFFICE

BUS GATES

OFFICE

TICKET BOOTH

ACCESS TO MBTA SUBWAY

RETAILS

KIOSKS

1900'S

While it was already the largest, South Station quickly became the busiest train station in the world, handling about 38 million passengers in 1913, ranking higher than its second nearest competitor, Boston's North Station, which handled 29 million and New York's Grand Central Station, which handled 22 million that same year.

The building also stands as a living museum of rail history with historic wall plaques documenting achievements in the station's history and even a wall exhibit featuring old South Station souvenir memorabilia. The station also features permanent art fixtures including Jeffrey Schiff's "Destinations" comprised of 25 cast bronze destination plumbs hung above the main entrance of the station and Mayer Spivak's "Muscle Bound for Miami" near the Amtrak information desk.

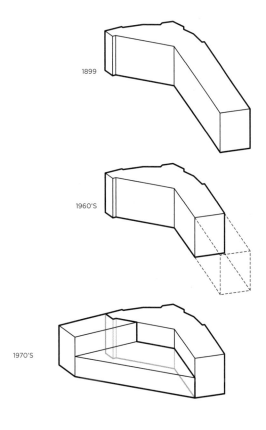

1899

1960'S

1970'S

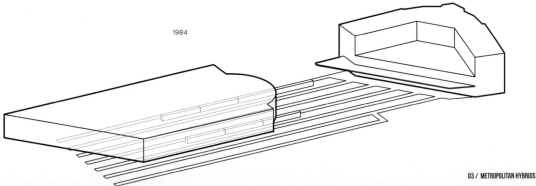

1984

NORTH STATION + TD GARDEN

ADDRESS: 100 LEGENDS WAY, BOSTON, MA

YEAR: 1995

PROGRAM: SPORTS ARENA

                MBTA COMMUTER RAIL STATION

                MBTA SUBWAY STATION

                RETAIL

                PARKING

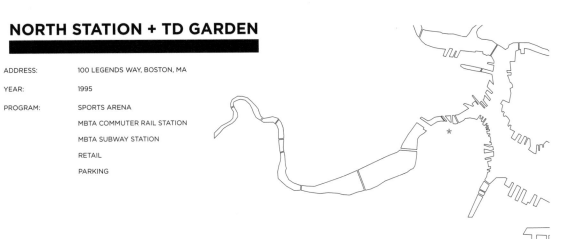

PARKING

MBTA RAILWAY STATION

MBTA ORANGE/GREEN LINE

RETAIL

SPORTS ARENA

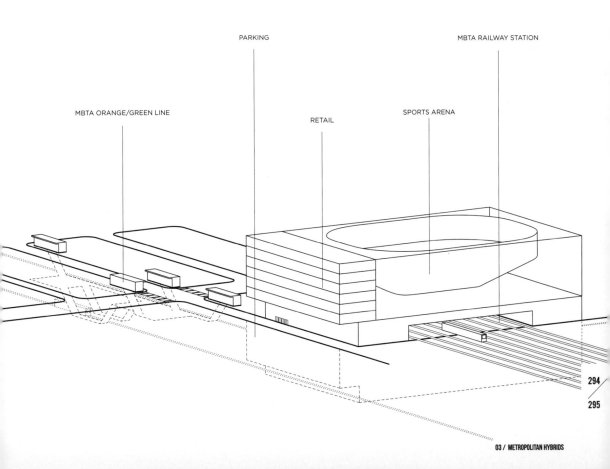

294
295

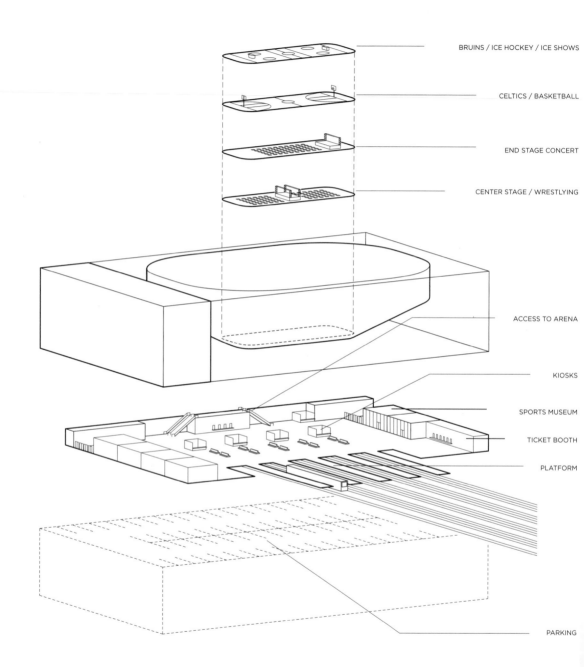

BRUINS / ICE HOCKEY / ICE SHOWS

CELTICS / BASKETBALL

END STAGE CONCERT

CENTER STAGE / WRESTLYING

ACCESS TO ARENA

KIOSKS

SPORTS MUSEUM

TICKET BOOTH

PLATFORM

PARKING

CELTICS / BASKETBALL

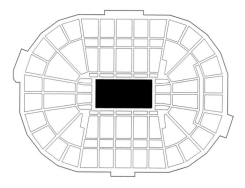

BRUINS / ICE HOCKEY / ICE SHOWS

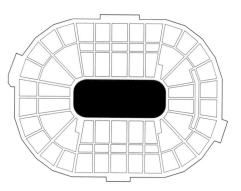

END STAGE CONCERT

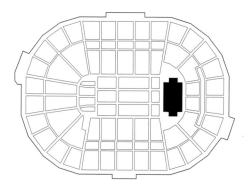

CENTER STAGE / WRESTLING

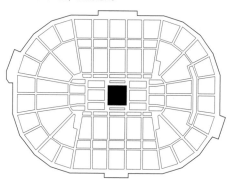

SYMPHONY GARAGE

ADDRESS: 41 WESTLAND AVENUE, BOSTON, MA

YEAR:

PROGRAM: PARKING

     CAR LIFT

     GROCERY

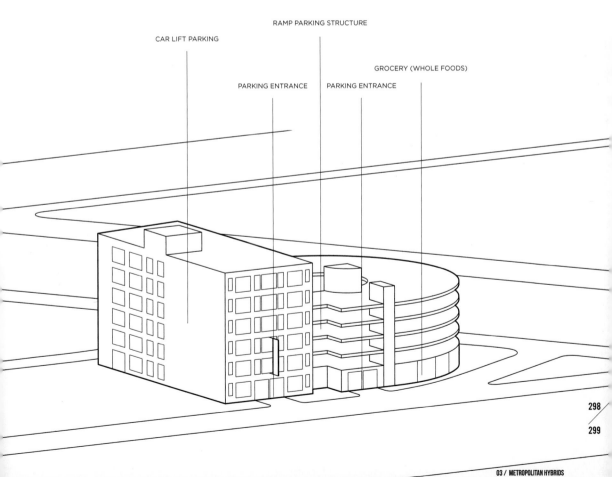

CAR LIFT PARKING

RAMP PARKING STRUCTURE

GROCERY (WHOLE FOODS)

PARKING ENTRANCE PARKING ENTRANCE

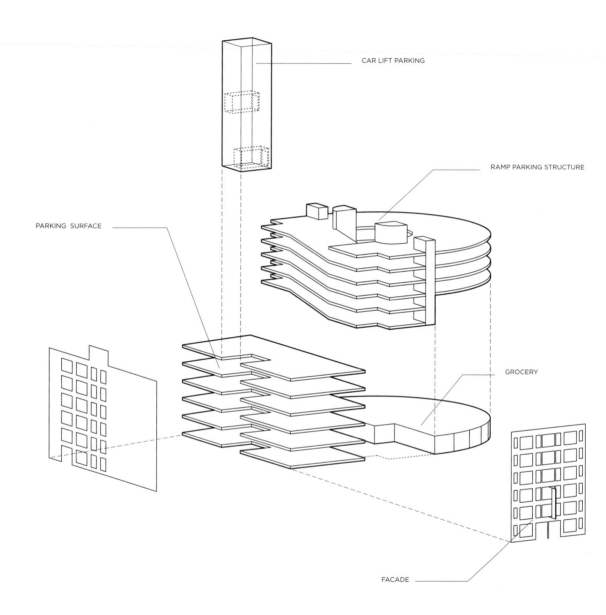

CAR LIFT PARKING

RAMP PARKING STRUCTURE

PARKING SURFACE

GROCERY

FACADE

RAMP PARKING

CAR LIFT

FACADE

300
301

SYMPHONY HOUSING

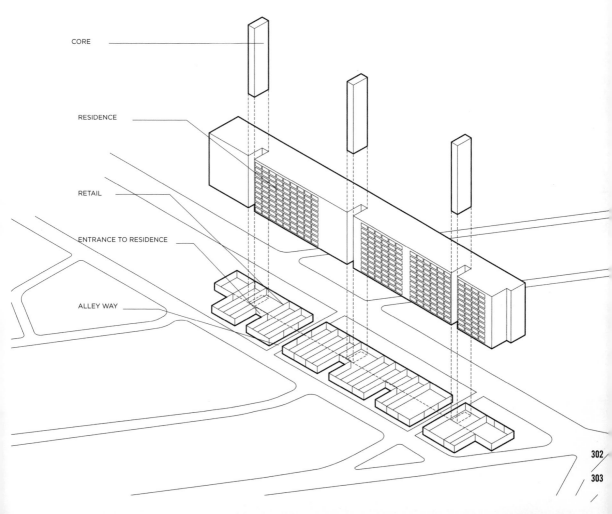

CORE

RESIDENCE

RETAIL

ENTRANCE TO RESIDENCE

ALLEY WAY

BOSTON COMMON PARKING

ADDRESS: ZERO CHARLES STREET, BOSTON, MA

YEAR:

PROGRAM: PARKING (UNDERGROUND)

                PARK

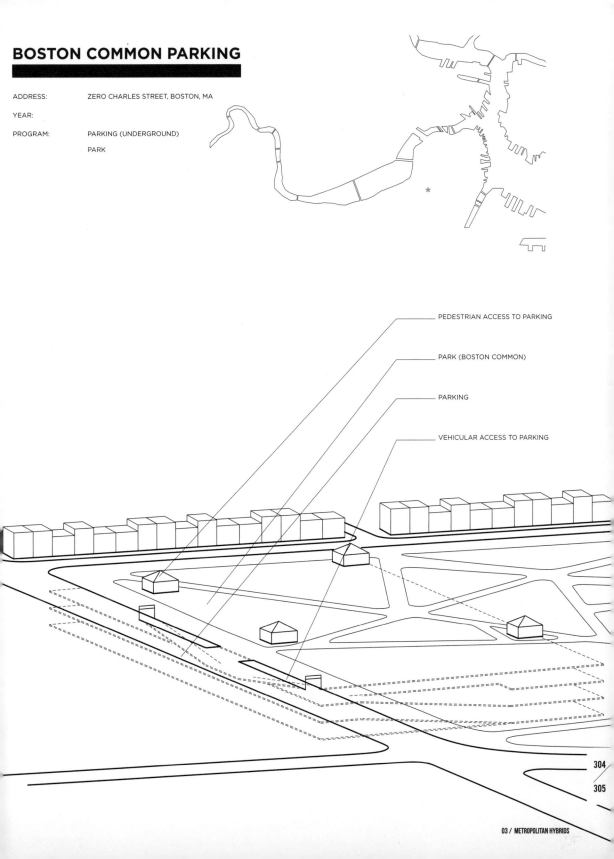

PEDESTRIAN ACCESS TO PARKING

PARK (BOSTON COMMON)

PARKING

VEHICULAR ACCESS TO PARKING

304

305

HARVARD SQUARE STATION

ADDRESS: 1400 MASSACHUSETTS AVENUE, CAMBRIDGE, MA

YEAR: 1912

PROGRAM: MBTA SUBWAY STATION

                MBTA BUS STOP(UNDERGROUND)

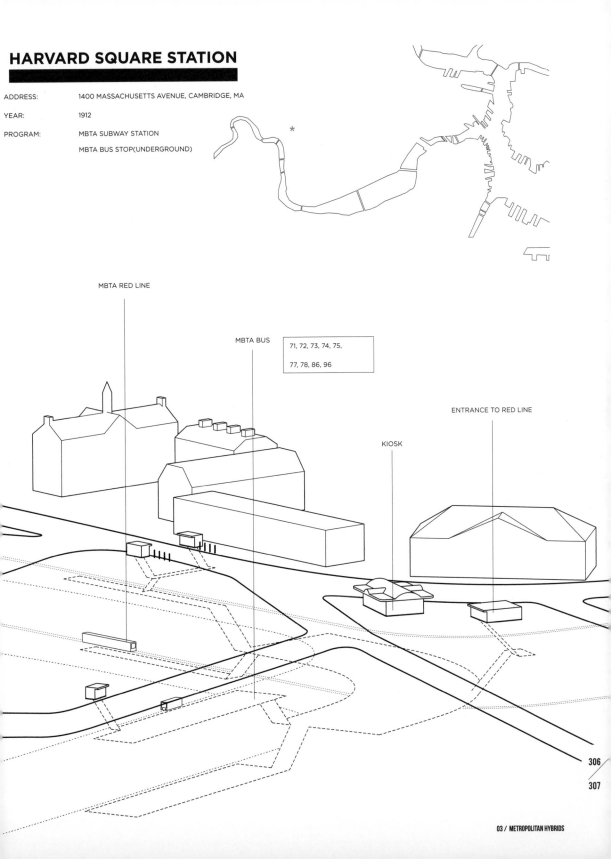

MBTA RED LINE

MBTA BUS

71, 72, 73, 74, 75,
77, 78, 86, 96

ENTRANCE TO RED LINE

KIOSK

306
307

The experience of the city is never static. Our sense of the urban environment and our ability to navigate its terrain are constantly negotiated, subject to the hidden process- es that influence the forms we see. Design plays an instrumental role in this translation. Physical interventions can help or hinder our understanding of a city's spaces, clarify or obscure its systems of movement, and en- able or deny the participation of its various publics. By framing the means through which we interpret and engage with our surround- ings, designers can reveal the changing as- pects of a city's present, tell stories about its past, and speculate on its future.

INFORM exhibition (at Boston Society of Architecture)

FICTION
BOSTON

In early 2012, the Boston Society of Architecture held an exhibition called "INFORM" in its new headquarters. The exhibition was about five major projects that have attempted to reshape the perception of Boston since the 1960s.

The future of the city, as envisioned by past Bostonians, was illuminating because we are, in some ways, living in the city that they had imagined. The 1960s was a period in architecture and urbanism when the wave of Modernism was still high and new technologies overwhelmed the built environment. Many cities in the United States started a morphological transformation during this period. Although the 1960s was a period of radical experimentation and intervention in many areas in the world, it was not only during the 1960s that Boston attempted a transformation. As the exhibition made evident, Boston has repeatedly tried to reshape its physical form. Fifty years later, what can we picture for the future of Boston? What kind of strategies will the city employ in the next fifty years?

In his article "Past Futures", Boston-based architect, Alex Krieger goes into more detail about what efforts Boston has undergone in the past in order to picture its future. He sees Boston as a city that always has been shaping newness with physical change. The physical environ-

A NEW APPROACH IS CALLED FOR ON THE WATERFRONT — ONE THAT IS BOTH MORE DELIBERATE AND MORE EXPERIMENTAL... THE MASSIVE EXPANSE OF THE SOUTH BOSTON WATERFRONT, WITH ITS EXISTING KNOWLEDGE BASE, OPPORTUNITY FOR GROWTH, AND WORLD-CLASS INFRASTRUCTURE IS RIPE TO PRODUCE WORLD-CLASS PRODUCTS AND SERVICES.

MAYOR THOMAS M. MENINO

//

CHARLES RIVER CONSERVANCY MASTER PLAN   SKATE PARK

ment we stand in at present is not the natural outcome of a non-interventionist strategy, but rather the result of a continuous process of changing the city with visionary plans. The efforts, of course, vary in scale from large land reclamations in the 17th century to infrastructural interventions with the integration of river and regional park system. It continues through urban projects such as the waterfront development, urban renewal, and a number of high-rise projects. The morphology of Boston is no accident but a result of past efforts and vision. This tells us that it is important to learn from the past and imagine a future for the next fifty years.

"A new approach is called for on the waterfront – one that is both more deliberate and more experimental... The massive expanse of the South Boston waterfront, with its existing knowledge base, opportunity for growth, and world-class infrastructure is ripe to produce world-class products and services."
Mayor Thomas M. Menino

As we have seen from Boston's history, future plans of the city are often pictured through reshaping the built environment. This is because the built environment, whether architectural or urban in scale, is an end result of our society; it incorporates technology, social demand, economy and culture. Boston presently has a number of major projects on going. Harvard's Allston Campus and the Innovation District in South Boston are two major projects that will reshape the city in the next twenty years. Both developments will not only influence the transformation of the city but will impact non-physical transformation by generating new jobs and new industries. Given the importance of the location,

the Innovation District will most likely stimulate development and growth in other districts as well. The district is around 1,000 acres in South Boston's waterfront area where the Boston Convention & Exhibition Center is located. Since 2010, when Mayor Menino announced the strategy for the district, the number of venture companies has grown, and the city of Boston is continuing its effort of inviting major companies and institutions to the district. Babson College, whose main campus is located in Wellesley, MA, recently launched its satellite campus in the district. Comparing this area with other institutional cores we have seen in chapter two offers an instructive juxtaposition. As a matter of fact, the Innovation District has the potential to address every metropolitan aspect we mention in the book, from the infrastructural level to urban core and architectural level. And perhaps, the district will be a framework or guideline for future growth in Boston.

Boston's efforts are also focused on keeping young professionals in the city after they graduate from Boston's many colleges and universities. Boston has countless students who will potentially become leading professionals in their various fields. However, Boston has a problem keeping them in the city, and lose many financial and business professionals to New York, information technology graduates to San Jose, and so on. As Boston faces the issue of how to keep them in the city, both the Innovation District and Harvard Allston Campus can play a role in providing new jobs and businesses in the city for new graduates.

Along with these large scale efforts on reshaping the morphology as well as socioeconomic conditions of

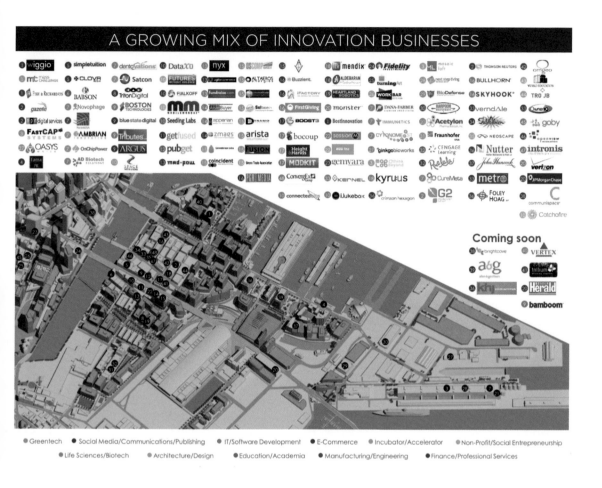

A GROWING MIX OF INNOVATION BUSINESSES

- ● Greentech
- ● Social Media/Communications/Publishing
- ● IT/Software Development
- ● E-Commerce
- ● Incubator/Accelerator
- ● Non-Profit/Social Entrepreneurship
- ● Life Sciences/Biotech
- ● Architecture/Design
- ● Education/Academia
- ● Manufacturing/Engineering
- ● Finance/Professional Services

MINI METROPOLIS ALSO NEEDS/DESERVES ITS OWN SPECIALIZED ARCHITECTURE THAT CAN VINDICATE THE ORIGINAL PROMISE OF THE MINI METROPOLITAN CONDITION AND FURTHER DEVELOP THE FRESH TRADITIONS OF THE CULTURE OF MINI METROPOLITANISM.

the city, there are smaller infrastructural efforts within the city. As mentioned before, Boston has a well established artificial and natural infrastructure. There have always been efforts to strengthen the use of them either through developments, or through reformation. For instance, as we saw in Chapter One, there are continuous efforts to use air-rights over the Massachusetts Turnpike as a means of stitching together the urban fabric. As part of a natural infrastructural effort, the Charles River is also being reformed with projects like the Charles River Skate Park, and cleaning the river to swimming standards. These efforts are not just for making the riverside more accessible but also for connecting different neighborhoods and communities together. For instance, the Charles River Skate Park project, to-

gether with neighboring parks, create a landscape network that connects East Cambridge, Charlestown and the West End neighborhoods of Boston.

Besides efforts that are currently being undertaken in Boston, what can we picture at present for the future Boston? Certainly, the picture should be creative and at times radical to reflect an ideal future. At the same time, the proposals should position themselves on the lineage of past efforts , which is the purpose of our analysis of the built environment in Boston through the eyes of the MINI Metropolis. The hidden argument of this research is that a MINI Metropolis needs its own architecture and urbanism. The strategy it utilizes should not be something adopted from other metropolises. Borrowing

DISTRICT STRATEGY WITHIN A CITY

BOSTON
INNOVATION DISTRICT
(SOUTH BOSTON)

0   5km

NEW YORK
ROOSEVELT ISLAND

0   5km

from Rem Koolhaas' expression about the metropolis, MINI Metropolis also needs/deserves its own specialized architecture that can vindicate the original promise of the MINI Metropolitan condition and further develop the fresh traditions of the culture of MINI Metropolitanism. Hence, the Fiction Boston would be sometimes radical like the 1960s proposals for Boston, sometimes big like Frederick Law Olmstead's Emerald Necklace, and sometimes realistic like any other proposals we see today. However, no matter the personality of each project, Fiction Boston is directly addressing the challenges of MINI Metropolitanism through different scales of projects and with unique strategies.

SINGLE INDUSTRY URBANIZATION

SAN MATEO

PALO ALTO

SANTA CLARA

SAN JOSE

SILICONE VALLEY
CAMPBELL, CUPERTINO, LOS ALTOS, LOS ALTOS HILLS, LOS GATOS, MILPITAS, MONTE SERENO, MORGAN HILL, MOUNTAIN VIEW, PALO ALTO, SAN JOSE, SANTA CLARA, SARATOGA, SUNNYVALE

0   5km

SMALL BUT BIG

The book "XS" tells us how big ideas can be implemented into small scale projects. It is true that the size of an idea is not the same as the size of the project. This simple fact can easily fit to the scale of urban impact. It is not only large-scale projects that have big impacts on the city; small-scale projects can influence at a city scale. Perhaps small scale projects may not be able to change the morphology of the city directly, but they can still introduce new ways of public interaction as part of urban activities. Eventually, the new urban interaction will catalyze various dialogues between the public and the city. In a way, it evokes the concept of the folly that Bernard Tschumi introduced with his Parc de la Villette project. There follies become a means of perception of space, and interaction between visitors and the park happen through the follies as an event.

This "small but big" project was investigated in the 1960s in Boston as well. An information center, designed by Ashley Myer Smith Architects was temporarily installed at Park Square as means of interaction between the public and the civic side of the city. People could ask questions and get answers in real-time. Illuminated inflatable balloons were another way of creating interaction with the city at night. Although it was a temporary installation for Signs/Lights/Boston, it was experimental enough to introduce a means of interaction and a new urban activity to the public. How might we re-interpret these ideas and adopt them for a future Boston?

WEST
END
PAVILION

This experimental way of interacting is something that the West End Pavilion engages. This project addresses two big issues: perception of neighborhood and public involvement. The West End is a neighborhood in Boston between the North End and Beacon Hill. Boston is very much a neighborhood-based city and each neighborhood has a very strong and unique character, not only in terms of culture, but also of built environment. For example, the North End is known as Little Italy filled with Italian restaurants, cafes, bakeries, churches, and narrow alleys. While many other neighborhoods in Boston are well know for certain characteristics, the West End is not well known to Bostonians, not to mention visitors to Boston. This is partly because the old fabric, which was more characteristically similar to Beacon Hill, and the North End was wiped

out as part of an urban renewal project in the 1950s and 60's. Since then the neighborhood has struggled to enhance its unique culture and reach out to other Bostonians.

As previously mentioned, one of the issues that this project addresses is the perception of neighborhood. We developed a hexagonal module that can be used as urban furniture as well as a medium for information. The surface of the module has engraved information about the West End, while it still can be used as bench or platform for the public. When people use this urban furniture they casually get information about the neighborhood, and more importantly, as the modules are able to be transported to other places, each module becomes a means of dialogue between neighborhoods. For instance, when modules get transported to different neighborhoods of Boston to provide resting benches for the public, they will come to reflect on the story of the West End. This is a way of enhancing people's familiarity with the West End.

Another aspect of the West End Pavilion is that people can actively get involved in forming the layout of furniture. Three different types

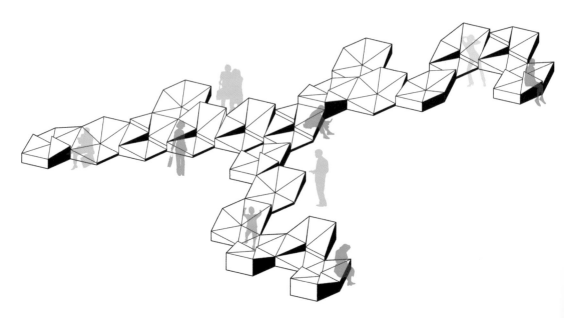

of modular unit let the pavilion form a variety of fields depending on how they are laid out. They can be clustered into sections, they can form a continuous field, and they can create a big platform depending on the purpose, site condition, and number of units. In the project, the involvement and interaction do not happen through digital media, which we see almost redundantly these days, they happen by physical touch: holding and pushing.

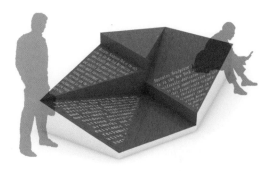

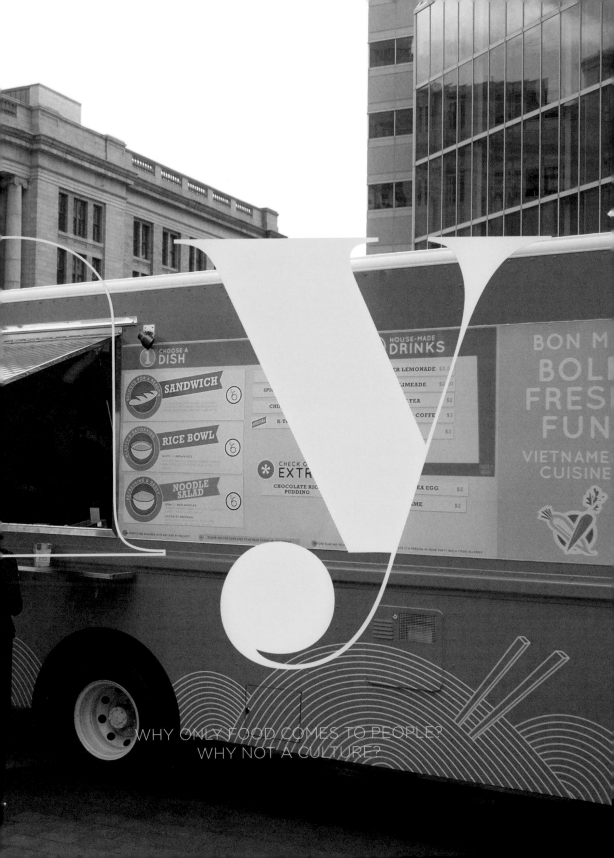

WHY ONLY FOOD COMES TO PEOPLE?
WHY NOT A CULTURE?

DESIGN MUSEUM BOSTON MOBILE GALLERY

Design Museum Boston Mobile Gallery also follows the idea of having bigger impact on the city and public through smaller scale projects. It is even more active than the West End Pavilion in that it does not reside in any one place. It travels around the city and actively engages the public instead of sitting in a place and waiting for the public to come to it. The mobile gallery is much like a food truck for design. Food trucks are not really a replacement for traditional restaurants, rather they are an alternative to bridge a gap. They provide a public alternative menu, price and place. The success of a food truck is not about it having a cheaper menu, but its active engagement of potential customers. The same concept is borrowed for Design Museum Boston Mobile Gallery. Design Museum Boston is not a replacement for a museum, it is an alternative

IT IS LIKE A   FOOD TRUCK FOR DESIGN

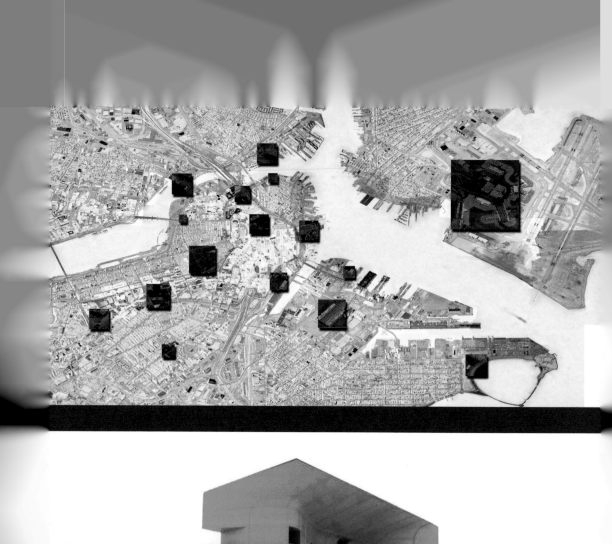

model for a museum that promotes design and Boston designers. Thus, it is very important for Design Museum Boston to reach out actively to a public who may not be aware of the museum. The mobile gallery is designed within the area constraints of one parking spot, so that it can be parked anywhere. After it's parked, the mobile truck becomes a gallery where people can come in and see the exhibition.

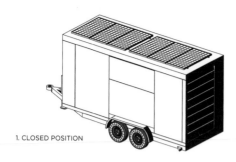

1. CLOSED POSITION

2. INFORMATION BOOTH

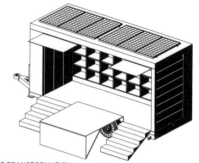

4. STAGE TRANSFORMATION

3. MUSEUM TRANSFORMATION

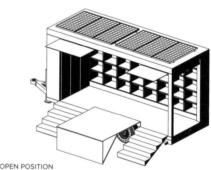

5. OPEN POSITION

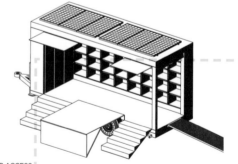

6. RAMP ACCESS

IT TRAVELS AROUND THE CITY AND ACTIVELY APPROACHES TO PUBLIC INSTEAD OF SITTING AT A PLACE AND WAITING FOR PUBLIC TO COME.

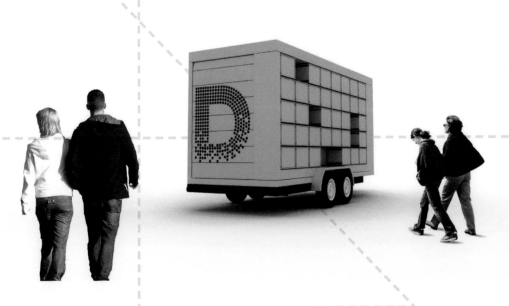

CATALYST

In most cities, whether big or small, booming or busting, dense or not, many key projects are often proposed to generate, or at times revitalize, urban development. These projects become a catalyst for the city in the sense that they have both direct and indirect influence on the morphology of the city. As described in "Integral Boston", these catalytic projects can be explored through key buildings or urban typologies, and will stimulate a new wave of urban activities such as culture, consumption, and interaction. Especially, as Joan Busquets mentions, key projects are not a large-scale projects in a city that looks symbolic but projects that generate new urban interactions in the city.

Catalytic projects are not a new strategy in Boston. The Prudential Center development meant to revitalize the core of the city, and more recently, the ICA was built as part of a generator for the Innovation District development. However, through the catalytic projects we propose here, we are attempting to address the issue of MINI Metropolitan architecture. With the architectural potential of hybrid projects we found in Boston, which was analyzed in chapter three, the new proposal will incorporate the features of Boston to go further towards MINI Metropolitan architecture.

can

CAN WE HAVE A MEGA HYBRID STRUCTURE TO
MAXIMIZE THE USE OF PUBLIC TRANSPORTATION
AND TO HAVE EFFICIENT WAY OF USING A LIMITED
LAND? WHAT IF NORTH STATION IN BOSTON
BECOMES LIKE KYOTO STATION?

HYBRID
STATION

As we saw in the previous chapter, North Station is already a unique hybrid project in that it integrates a commuter rail station with a sports arena. However, if we develop on the surface parking lot right next to the arena, we can enhance the hybridity of the building so that it acts as a catalyst for new types of urban activities in the city and more immediate in the West End neighborhood. Kyoto Station, which is an extremely successful hybrid building in a traditional city, provides a variety of activities in the building that cannot be easily achieved in other parts of the city. Similar in strategy to Kyoto Station, Hybrid Station creates urban life in the building. It is a space where people shop, commute, reside, stay temporarily, congregate, work, and participate in cultural activities. Yet, it is not simply a mega-mixed use building. Because it transforms itself to accom-

modate each urban activity, instead of letting the program fit to the box, it is more accurately designated a hybrid building.

Hybrid Station also generates a conversation about maximizing the use of the station and nearby area. More and more people commute by public transportation, especially in Boston, and it is promoted as a component of sustainable urban living. However, few attempts have been made to address this issue physically, and thus, the built environment remains the same while urban life changes. Hybrid Station not only densifies North Station, but also multiplies its layers of use. It is also a strategy of introducing hierarchy of density in urban space in relation to public transportation. In a MINI Metropolis, where, unlike a mega-metropolis, not all areas can be dense, there should be a way of densifying specific areas so that the rest of the city can maintain certain levels of density. In short, Hybrid Station provides enough room for a condominium, office, hotel, and restaurants, etc. in a lot of limited capacity that is integrated into a public transit-oriented urban life.

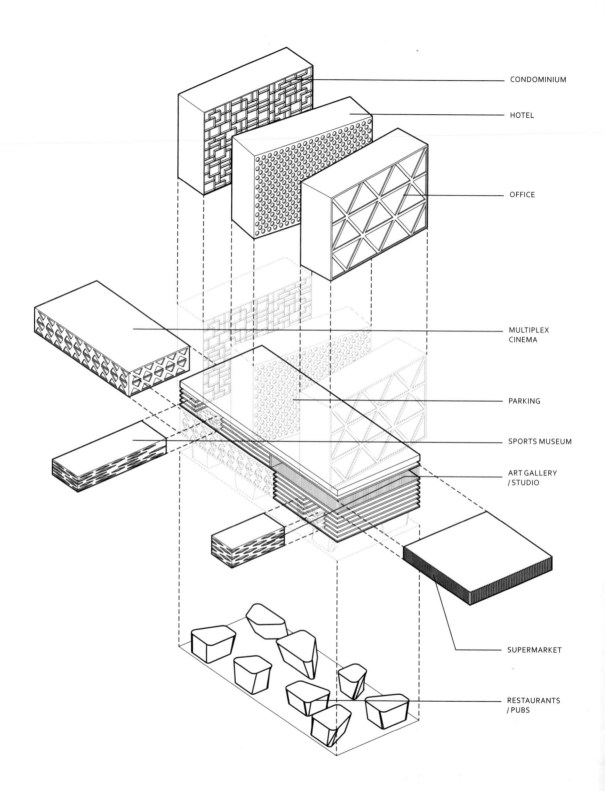

CONDOMINIUM

HOTEL

OFFICE

MULTIPLEX
CINEMA

PARKING

SPORTS MUSEUM

ART GALLERY
/ STUDIO

SUPERMARKET

RESTAURANTS
/ PUBS

we

CAN WE THINK OF A MAJOR CATALYTIC PROJECT
THAT CAN STIMULATE BOTH PHYSICAL AND
ECONOMICAL TRANSFORMATION OF THE AREA?
WHAT WOULD BE THE STRATEGY TO GENERATE
NEW TYPES OF BUSINESS AND INDUSTRY
INSTEAD OF JUST INCREASING RENTABLE SPACE?
WITH HAVING MORE THAN 4.7 MILLION VISITORS
A YEAR. TATE MODERN DID NOT ONLY
GENTRIFIED THE BUILDING BUT ALSO CATALYZED
OTHER DEVELOPMENTS AROUND THE AREA.

TATE
BOSTON

Tate Boston is a proposal for a catalytic project in Boston. It is a similar strategy to Guggenheim Bilbao or Tate Modern London in that it attempts to stimulate larger urban development. Tate Modern London brings in 4.7 million visitors a year and influences other development around the area. The site for Tate Boston was chosen with this in mind. The site is not only a former industrial area that needs to be redeveloped but also in a location where Charlestown, East Boston and Chelsea meet. The expected redevelopment of the area, catalyzed by Tate Boston, will become an area that links those three different neighborhoods. By having the location accessible from the river, it will also generate higher use of water transportation systems.

Going back to MINI Metropolitan architecture, the Tate Boston proposal is a showcase for using an established built environment in new ways. Of course, converting old factories to luxury condominiums, or office space is not

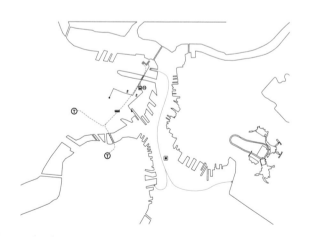

AFTER

a new concept, even in Boston where factories and warehouses in the Waterfront and South Boston have been converted. However, what can we do in addition to just providing additional floor area in the city? The effort of a developer to convert an old factory to condominiums ends with that single building. The role of a catalytic project like the Tate Boston, is to promote further development in the area by renovating a key building, somewhat like urban acupuncture.

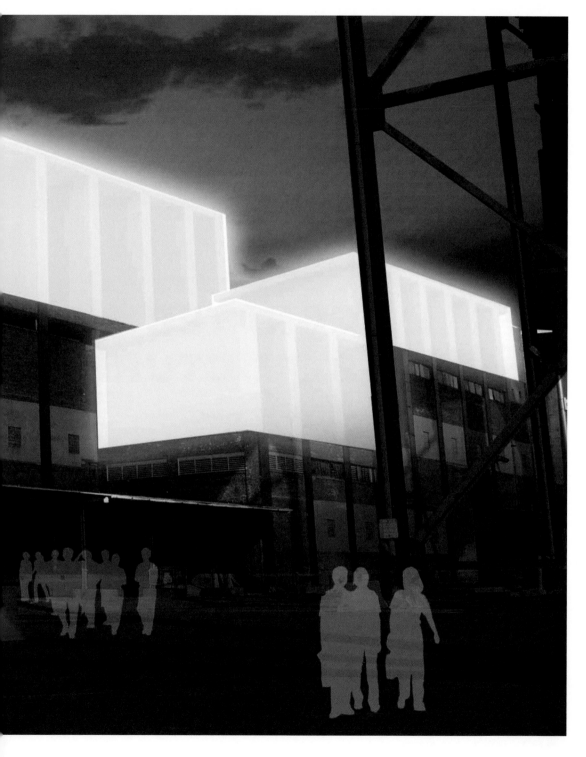

344
345

INTEGRATED INFRASTRUCTURE

Boston cannot be understood without its major networks of infrastructure, not just highways and transportation routes, but its landscape and waterways networks. The history of Boston can be understood as the history of land reclamation, and an early infrastructural effort for a planned landscape infrastructure, Olmstead's Emerald Necklace, not only to enrich the quality of life in Boston, but also to form the city and connect neighborhoods through the landscape. The infrastructure put in place throughout Boston's history provides the platform for future development.

One example of infrastructure integrated development is Boston's I-90 highway air-rights, which are being given to link the separated fabric of the city like the South End to the Back Bay and Chinatown. Another example is the Big Dig project, in which each reclaimed parcel of land has been developed as park space with public programming. Seeing the amount of energy given to infrastructure driven development, perhaps we can begin to think about more clever ways of introducing new infrastructure. While the scale might not be the same in all cases, other hybrid projects in Boston that are integrated with infrastructure might give us clues for potential strategies regarding Integrated Infrastructure.

GREEN LOOP BOSTON

Just as Boston Common integrated large-scale parking infrastructure, Green Loop Boston also integrates transit-oriented infrastructure by introducing a light rail system over a landscape network. Boston's park system has been in development since the 18th century with the Emerald Necklace project, and through the 19th century with the addition of numerous community parks. Most recently it has seen the development of the Green Way over the now underground I-93 Highway that cuts through the city. Green Loop Boston is

landscape and infrastructural effort designed to stitch together into a singular loop the various parts of the park system that have been added in the past two centuries.

This regional scale park system would not be the Boston area's first. In fact, Charles Eliot and Sylvester Baxter formed the Metropolitan Park system in the 1890s, which extends North to Winchester, West to Wellesley, and South to Milton. It was part of an effort to make Boston more metropolitan. Green Loop Boston would

next

FROM THE EMERALD NECKLACE IN 1800S TO GREEN WAY IN
2000'S, BOSTON PUT MUCH EFFORT TO PROVIDE ENOUGH
GREEN SPACES IN THE CITY AS WELL AS TO ENHANCE THE
LIVING QUALITY OF NEIGHBORHOODS THROUGH THEM. THEN
WHAT IS THE NEXT STEP AFTERWARDS?

cover a smaller area than the Metropolitan Park system. It would link Boston, Somerville, Cambridge, and Brookline for a total length of 30km. This would provide a similar length to the first outer ring of Paris, which is 35km. It would loop the area where the current MBTA network is poorly integrated with each other, and would provide a continuous path for biking and hiking. And as we can assume from the size of inner Paris, to the extent of its first perimeter ring, Green Loop Boston could provide new perspective on the area of Boston beyond its administrative boundary.

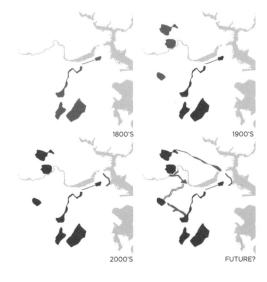

1800'S   1900'S

2000'S   FUTURE?

CAN WE THINK OF A NEW TYPE OF BUILDING
THAT PROVIDES AS MUCH AREA AS HIGH-RISE
BUILDINGS YET ADDRESSES ISSUES THAT CITY
IS FACING NOW?
IF THERE IS ANY, WHAT WOULD BE THE
SOCIAL RESPONSIBILITY OF A BUILDING?

BOSTON WATERFRONT RING

Like Green Loop Boston, which tries to link separated neighborhoods, the Boston Waterfront Ring also addresses the issue of how architecture, or infrastructure can respond to socioeconomic issues in the city. Currently, Boston has a number of skyscrapers planned for the near future, and the total floor area between them is nearly four times bigger than the area of central Boston. However, as Rem Koolhaas once insisted, building footprints keep increasing but the intensity of use is decreasing. If we admit that his assertion is fact and reconsider what would increase intensity of use in the future, we might come up with more creative and radical, but still practicable solution.

The Boston Waterfront Ring connects three distinct neighborhoods of Boston: central Boston, East Boston and Charlestown. Although they are physically very close to each other, unbelievably, there is no pedestrian or bike connection from East Boston to central Boston, or Charlestown to East Boston. This simple condition causes issues of socio-demographic segregation. The Boston Waterfront Ring is a major infrastructural effort to resolve this issue with the integration of housing, transportation, and public programs, meant to increase the connectivity and activities between these three areas. As a matter of fact, a similar effort can be found in the 1911 project, "An Island for the Charles River," by Arthur A. Shurtleff. The project is essentially a bridge on the Charles River between Cambridge and Boston along Massachusetts Ave , and integrates an artificial island between the cities. Locating buildings on the island would allow the infrastructure to become an active connection between the two cities. Although the way it integrated infrastructure with program is different from the Boston Waterfront Ring, the to proposals share similar concepts of utilizing infrastructure with a larger civic role.

MULTI-USED CITY

As cities become more globalized, and local governments get stronger, the global strength of a city has become an important topic. Cites are spending time and energy to host international level sporting events, cultural events and festivals. There is a common understanding that competition is not only between nations but also between world-class cities, and through these international events, a city can benefit from advantages such as increased tourism, which can potentially generate growth and development in the city. It is also true that many international events become generators of future growth patterns in a city. For instance, when the Olympic Games were held in Seoul, Korea in 1988, it also stimulated enormous development in a part of the city that was previously under-developed before the Olympics, as well as changed the perception of the country on the world stage.

Surprisingly enough, Boston has never hosted any major international event in its history. While four Summer Olympic Games, and four Winter Olympic Games have been held in the United States, Boston has never been given the chance to host the games. Even international film festivals, like Toronto's International Film Festival or Festival de Cannes, which require less infrastructural investment, have never been held in Boston. Of course, Boston still manages to host around twenty million visitors a year to the city without those international events. If we understand the big picture of those events as strengthening the competitiveness of the city, perhaps we can think of international events not just for the purpose of increasing the number of visitors, but as part of an effort to enhance the quality of the city. Perhaps we can conceive of more creative strategies to accommodate international events in a MINI Metropolis using the existing built environment.

SHANGHAI EXPO

IS HOLDING AN OLYMPIC
IN BOSTON EVEN POSSIBLE?

BOSTON OLYMPIC 2020

As we have seen from many other Olympic cites throughout history, the Olympic Games, one of the biggest sporting events in the world, stimulates massive development, and new infrastructure. In many cases, it becomes a good strategy to boost the economy and attract new construction in underdeveloped areas of the city. However, it is also true that many cities struggle with the use of new large-scale infrastructure projects like arenas, and stadiums after the games. This could prove an unhappy legacy should Boston ever hold the Olympic Games. One question is whether Boston even has the necessary infrastructure to hold an Olympic Games.

To answer that question, we should not overlook the number of sports facilities

BOSTON HAVE MORE THAN ENOUGH FACILITIES TO ACCOMMODATE OLYMPIC GAMES, AND MOST OF THEM HAVE OLYMPIC QUALIFIED SIZE

owned by the major universities in Boston and professional sports stadiums in the city. As we saw in the second chapter, there are 35 higher education institutions in administrative Boston and 54 in regional Boston. Eight of them have greater than ten thousand students, which means that universities in Boston could potentially have more than enough facilities to accommodate an Olympic games. Most of the sports facilities are even of Olympic qualified size, and that's not to mention professional facilities, like Fenway Park and TD Garden. Thus, it may be necessary to construct only a few new pieces of infrastructure. Aside from arenas and stadiums, a fair amount of accommodation is needed to hold an Olympic Games. This could also potentially be satisfied with the housing facilities of the universities. Since the Games are usually held for two weeks in the summer, when most students are on break, it would not be a big conflict to use school affiliated housing as accommodation for athletes. Boston might be able to hold an Olympic Games in the near future without major investment, after all.

Image MassGIS Commonwealth of Massachusetts EOEA

OLYMPIC VS. BOSTON MARATHON

11,000

AVERAGE ATHLETES
ATTENDING IN OLYMPICS

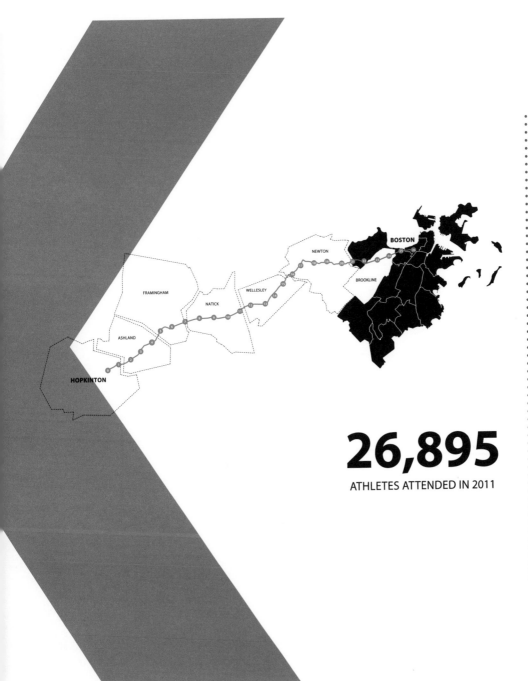

BOSTON

NEWTON

FRAMINGHAM

WELLESLEY

BROOKLINE

NATICK

ASHLAND

HOPKINTON

26,895
ATHLETES ATTENDED IN 2011

WHAT ABOUT SPORTS FACILITIES?

TOGETHER WITH PROFES-
SIONAL SPORTS FACILITIES
LIKE, FENWAY PARK AND
TD GARDEN, COLLEGES IN
BOSTON AREA HAVE MORE
THAN ENOUGH NUMBERS OF
OLYMPIC QUALITY FACILITIES
ALREADY, INCLUDING 30,000
SEATING CAPACITY OF HAR-
VARD STADIUM AND OLYMPIC
SIZE BLODGETT POOl.

Boston College HS
Boston College
Boston University
Fenway Park
Harvard University
MIT
Northeastern University
TD Garden
TUFTS University
University of Massachusetts

OLYMPIC IS MOSTLY HELD IN JULY AND AUGUST FOR ABOUT 2 WEEKS WHEN COLLEGE STUDENTS ARE OUT FOR VACATION.

37,000
STUDENTS IN ON-CAMPUS FACILITIES

11,000
DORMITORY BEDS ADDED SINCE 2000

2,200
ADDITIONAL BEDS IN PLAN

WHAT ABOUT ACCOMMODATIONS?

CAN BOSTON HOLD AN EXPO WITHOUT TAKING OUT A
MASSIVE LAND LIKE SHANGHAI?

THE SHANGHAI WORLD EXPO WAS ALSO THE LARGEST WORLD'S FAIR SITE
EVER AT 5.28 SQUARE KM. BY THE END OF THE EXPO, OVER 73 MILLION
PEOPLE HAD VISITED - A RECORD ATTENDANCE - AND 250 COUNTRIES AND
INTERNATIONAL ORGANIZATIONS HAD PARTICIPATED. ON OCTOBER 16, 2010,
THE EXPO SET A SINGLE-DAY RECORD OF HAVING OVER 1.03 MILLION VISI-
TORS ENTER THE EXHIBITION THAT DAY.

BOSTON 2020 WORLD EXPO

X X

I WANT TO BE METROPOLITAN

BOSTON EXPO 2020

The World Exposition is another major international event that is city-based. Since it was first held in 1851 in London, it has required a large designated area so that nations can build pavilions to showcase their technology and culture. Although the contents of the exhibitions in those pavilions have changed throughout the decades, the concept of having a large empty site to accommodate them has remained the same. As we saw from the Shanghai Expo in 2010, a massive land area was developed just to hold the expo. Although parts of it will be developed into new housing, the strategy is not very sustainable. Similar to Olympic infrastructure, pavilions become problematic environments after the event's completion. It is not surprising then to see MVRDV's amazing Dutch pavilion at Hannover Expo in 2000 become an abandoned slum. It is not because of the architecture, but rather because of the concept of a large site on the outskirts of the city, which becomes isolated after the event that the pavilions can become derelict.

Is there a way of holding an Expo without creating this unfortunate condition? Actually, Boston had developed a proposal for a World Exposition in 1976. Architect, Jan Wampler proposed an experimental project that would float the fair in the water. This radical project was not just for the Expo but also addressed a new way of growing and developing the city. What can we learn from this project? And what would we need to consider in hosting an Expo in the 21st century?

Perhaps, designating one large-scale swath of land to accommodate the many pavilions is not a smart strategy, especially these days when sustainability is a key feature in development. What we might think of is distribution rather than concentration. If we consider the whole of Boston as a big canvas that we can play with, rather than one designated site, we would be able to distribute each nation's pavilion throughout different neighborhoods. We can use pocket spaces, abandoned sites, and surface parking lots to locate pavilions, and perhaps they could even be coordinated with the demographics of each neighborhood in Boston. For instance, East Boston, where the Latin population rate is very high, can invite pavilions from Latin American countries, while the North End, Boston's Little Italy, can host the Italian pavilion. As the pavilions would relate to the culture of the neighborhood, they could potentially be used as neighborhood museums, similar to West End Museum, which

I WANT TO BE METROPOLITAN

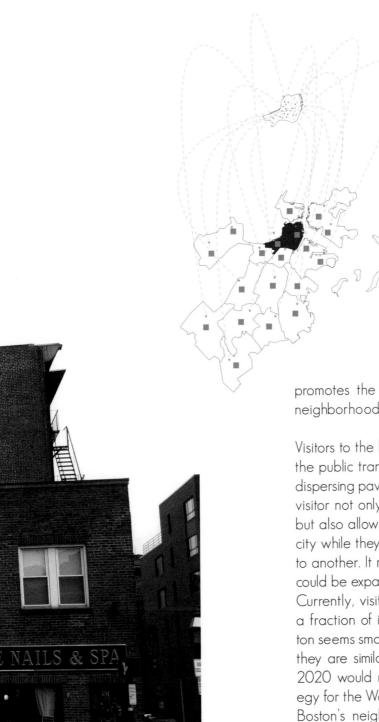

promotes the culture and the history of the neighborhood and enhances the community.

Visitors to the Expo can reach all pavilions via the public transportation system (MBTA). Thus, dispersing pavilions throughout the city lets the visitor not only see different nations' pavilions but also allows them to experience the whole city while they are traveling from one pavilion to another. It means the perception of Boston could be expanded far beyond what it is now. Currently, visitors perceive Boston to be only a fraction of its true area, which is why Boston seems smaller than inner Paris even though they are similar in size. In short, Boston Expo 2020 would not only introduce a new strategy for the World Exposition but also enhance Boston's neighborhood communities and expand the perception of the city.

I WANT TO BE METROPOLITAN

	HANNOVER	AICHI	ZARAGOZA	SHANGHAI
	2000	2005	2008	2010

AREA (KM2)

0.6	1.0	0.6	5.3

**VISITORS
(MILLION)**

25	23	20	73

20 MIL
NUMBER OF VISITORS A YEAR

5.7 KM2
CENTRAL BOSTON AREA

WHAT COULD BE THE SUSTAINABLE STRATEGY TO USE EXISTING STRUCTURE OF THE CITY AND STRENGTHEN IDENTITY OF EACH NEIGHBORHOOD?

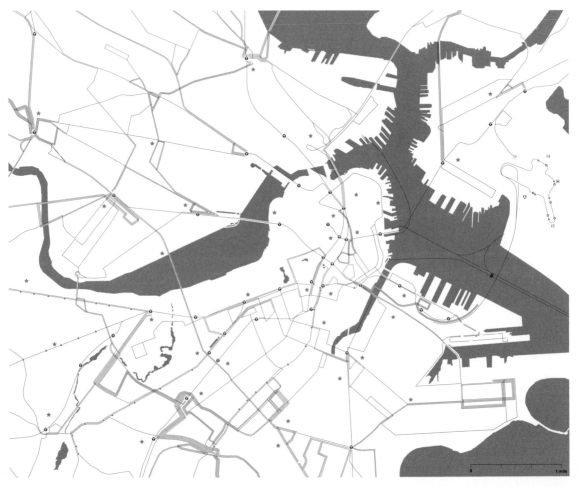

INCRE-MENTAL GROWTH IN MINI METROPO-LIS

BY: DONGWOO YIM

Since the emergence of modern architecture in the early 20th century, the discourse on the "city" has become one of the most important and interesting in the field of architecture. The onset of the modern era demanded a new type of lifestyle and a new type of city structure that could accommodate these new paradigms. Because of their ability to grapple with the challenge of changing physical environments, culture and technology, it was the architects that took on the task of building a new type of city. Numerous discussions about the "urban" continue today and more importantly a variety of ways of reading a city, which we may call "urbanism," are being proposed by numbers of architects/urbanists. The proposed "urbanisms" are not meant to designate what is right or wrong; instead they are largely subjective perspectives on how one can analyze a city and what one proposes for a city based on such perspectives. Different perspectives on a city can bring out different results of built environments. Thus, how we will approach Boston, or more specifically, which urbanism we will take on Boston, is the fundamental question that needs to be answered before proposing morphological change of Boston.

Before discussing urbanism, it is worth clarifying the architect's role in structuring a city. Is it to rationalize infrastructures? Or is it to distribute zoning or programming in a logical way? Unlike urban planning, which is a more analytical and statistical way of structuring a city and has numbers of different professions involved, urban design that is more or less in the architects' field can be defined as forming the actual physicality of urban space from the scale of a single block to the city level based on their perspectives. Hence, various types of urbanisms, especially those that are very subjective, are more related to urban design rather than to urban planning, which is a more rationalized objective field. In urban design, the architect mostly deals with three types of conditions to create spatial quality in urban scale: architecture, landscape and infrastructure. The influence of infrastructure is not only limited to physical roads, rails, or

380
381

EMPLOYING THE PERSPECTIVE OF INTEGRAL URBANISM WHILE READING BOSTON DOES NOT INTEND TO SKETCH AN ALIEN MASTER PLAN FOR THE FUTURE. RATHER, IT STRIVES TO UNDERSTAND THE EXISTING ECONOMY, CULTURE, AND SOCIETY BETTER AND FORESEE HOW A NEW FLOW OF DEMANDS CAN ACCOMMODATE THEM

"

bridges, but it also includes the existing fabric of the city. In all architectural or urban projects, project sites tend to lack existing fabrics. Thus they become the elements that architects cannot ignore just as they cannot remove infrastructures as they want. In this context, Stan Allen has insisted on the importance of infrastructures for providing direction for future development of a city as being flexible and anticipatory factor. Thus, the term "urbanism" highlights the importance of understanding the perspective that takes its own path by engaging architecture, landscape and infrastructure.

A number of "urbanisms" can be listed, and even a greater number of professionals are currently reinterpreting them in their own ways. From Kelvin Lynch's cognitive way of understanding a city, Rem Koolhaas' rationalized way of reading a city, Le Corbusier's architectural sketches, to Ebenezer Howard's diagram sketches for a new city, there are various kind of "urbanisms" on the table. Some urbanisms are based on how you "see" a city, some are on how you "read" it, and some are on how you "form" it. But when we look at the taxonomy of urbanism, the most important factor that becomes the standard of categorizing is the treatment of the existing fabric--the infrastructure. As mentioned above, dealing with infrastructure is directly related to the future of a city and sketching a future city, no matter how you define future (be it the next 10 years or centuries thereafter), would be the essence of urbanism. And when we see how previous architectures and landscapes have become existing conditions, infrastructure, in the present or in the future, it is not hard to see the importance of infrastructure in such an urbanism. Hence, the more important issue on urbanism is not only how you analyze a city but also how you understand and treat urban infrastructure, and urbanism can be described not only as a methodology but also as a paradigm that becomes your framework when you sketch a city. In short, the way how you define, treat, and suggest infrastructure is the key word that differentiates one urbanism from another.

Therefore, a variety of different urbanisms can be narrowed down to two based on how they treat urban infrastructure. One type preserves infrastructure and the other ignores it. Preserving infrastructure implies that the infrastructure itself has its own meaning, being the physical product of culture, technology, and public demands of the society; thus, it has enough value to be sustained in some way. On the other hand, an urbanism that tends to ignore existing infrastructure puts more value on the other things. This does not mean that the type of urbanism does not accept infrastructure as a physical product of a society, but rather that it tries to create a new infrastructural logic for a new society. It is based on the argument that existing infrastructure cannot accommodate new culture, technology, and public demands. In both cases, however, one idea they share is that of "changing" a city based on new demands. As mentioned above, an "urbanism" implies a meaning of proposing a new city. In this context of change, preservation can be reinterpreted as the transformation of existing infrastructure, and ignoring can be understood as proposing a new logic on a tabula rasa structure to reflect new demands.

In the modern era, various urbanisms emerged in the face of new paradigms as seen in periods such as Le Corbusier's "Plan Voisin," Tony Garnier's "Industrial City," and Ebenezer Howard's "Garden City." All that fall under this umbrella can be categorized as "ignoring" infrastructure. Because the paradigm shift was so radical, it seemed that the new structure for the period could not be dealt with using pre-existing conditions, just as the new paradigm had to take over all that came before it. New technology, new philosophies, and a new society in this era stimulated the public to seek a new environment as well. This atmosphere undeniably influenced the new urbanisms. The idea was to sketch or propose a city based completely on new paradigms as an imaginary city without any concerns about existing conditions. The advantage was that the concept of reflecting a new paradigm could be maintained without being manipulated by the existing condition. And it provides as a way of achieving a "utopia" through a newly built environment, and therefore, the new idea is appreciated more than the existing structure.

On the other hand, an urbanism that tends to preserve infrastructure mainly emerged in the period of postmodernism. After the strong wave of Modernism during the early 20th century, there was a move to criticize perspectives that rationalized and objectified every value in various field from the 1950s, though from the 1970s. Rather, proponents tried to accept subjective characters in each value. This movement, of course, influenced urbanisms as well. The tabula rasa type of urbanism can be understood as a very rationalized urbanism that is not subject to any existing condition, whereas an urbanism that tends to preserve existing infrastructure accommodates various conditions of infrastructure. In this latter type of urbanism, existing infrastructure, even when it is seen as problematic, is the condition that contains its own character and advantage of the city instead of the one that has to be ignored or removed. For instance, in his case study of Caracas, the community leader Francisco Perez argues that the "informality" of the city that challenges the notion of an 'ad-hoc' type master plan is more flexible than one that is "controlled" by the author. In a rationalized form of urbanism, mostly informal settlement is understood as a cause of urban congestion that must be replaced by a new type of urban morphology. However, as Perez suggests, in the perspective of informal urbanism, this comprises the nucleus of a city that has been layered for decades so that, even when development and urban transformation happens, it has to sit on top of those layers instead of removing all the layers that came before.

In the 1960s, against the backdrop of postmodernism, a significant theory of "relative" urbanism was established by Jane Jacobs. In her first publication "The Death and Life of Great American Cities," Jacobs points out that a city is an organism that can be sustained by organic relations between constituents. She goes on to argue that the organism that we see now is not the one that has to be removed but preserved and developed to live in a new environment. Although many "absolute" type of urbanisms were introduced by various architects such as Superstudio and Archigram, the 1960s proved to be a period between the Modern and Postmodern most architectural experiments and debates arose. Jacobs' idea of understanding a city as organism that we have to live with influenced most urbanisms that came after and tended to appreciate existing infrastructures. Interestingly, both Archigram and Jacobs approached a city as an organism in the same period, yet their approaches were very different. Unlike Archigram, which emphasized the organic features of the city and envisioned a futuristic machine-driven age, Jacobs opposed the master plan type development that was based in the machine age. Instead, she argued that organic interventions based on the existing fabric could transform the city in the face of new demands and changes. Later, this concept was developed in many other ways such as soft urbanism, post-urbanism, everyday urbanism and so on. Integral Urbanism also can be categorized in this group of urbanism for its character of overlaying one infrastructure on top of the other rather than replacing one while discarding the other. As opposed to the tabula rasa type of absolute master plan, this urbanism can be described as "incremental transformation" or "integral growth" as Nan Ellin defines in her book,"Integral Urbanism".

In Integral Urbanism, organic intervention is a catalyst in a city. It is not a master plan that changes the whole logic of the city nor a single artifact that does not have enough impact on the city to transform it. It is a catalyst that works on an architectural or urban mode that stimulates urban transformation and influences the future morphology of the city and yet does not change its most fundamental structure. This catalytic urban intervention can be achieved in two ways: through iconic projects and through typological interventions. Iconic projects in a city can stimulate non-physical factors such as market trends, public flows, and cultural activities, whereas typological interventions influence the city in a physical way through defining relationships between buildings and the environment. The Guggenheim Museum Bilbao, which has now become the most cited precedent for the urban catalytic project, is an iconic project. This key building is described by Joan Busquets as having the potential to make an impact on large scale urban transformation through synthetic gestures between 'iconic' architecture itself and its context. This urban impact is the key factor that differentiates catalytic project from other artifacts.

Typological intervention is another way of transforming the morphology of a city. Unlike an iconic project which directly impacts the existing context, a typological intervention may have less impact on surrounding fabric but nevertheless have an indirect influence when a series of those typologies are aggregated together. In an urban scale, typological intervention (a three-dimensionally built form that is influenced by the relationship between architecture and urban environment) works as a guide-liner for other surrounding developments so that their integration can eventually transform the morphology of the city and create a new relationship between built and natural environments. Hence, this approach is more about structuring open space, landscape, and infrastructure on an urban scale by introducing three-dimensional forms of architecture. For instance, with careful composition of nine different buildings on a 12-acre site, Rockefeller Center in Manhattan was able to create a new type of urban space within the standard Manhattan grid system. Although each piece of architecture may not be as significant as other iconic landmarks in Manhattan, the project had a huge morphological impact on the city as well as on the concept of 'urban space.'

In short, employing the perspective of Integral Urbanism while reading Boston does not intend to sketch an alien master plan for the future. Rather, it strives to understand the existing economy, culture, and society better and foresee how a new flow of demands can accommodate them. In addition insistence to appreciate the existing structure of the city intact, the economic scale of exemplifies the incremental growth of the city that is not far from radical. Unlike the examples of fast growing cities in Asia and Latin America, Boston most likely will have gradual growth just as it has been throughout its history. And this growth pattern will show how a MINI Metropolis can have its own strategy of growing that differs from mega-metropolis and fast growing cities.

THE TERM "URBANISM" HIGHLIGHTS THE IMPORTANCE OF UNDERSTANDING THE PERSPECTIVE THAT TAKES ITS OWN PATH BY ENGAGING ARCHITECTURE, LANDSCAPE AND INFRASTRUCTURE.

TALKING BOSTON

PHONE MEETING WITH **JAN WAMPLER**

PROFESSOR AT THE MIT SCHOOL OF ARCHITECTURE

BY RAFAEL LUNA

I spoke today with Jan Wampler, one of my professors from MIT, regarding the possibilities for a World Expo in Boston. Back in school in 2008, I remember him talking briefly about his proposal for a Boston Expo during the 1960's. Three years later, I happen to stumble upon his proposal for such project exhibited at the Boston Society of Architect. Since we are proposing a Boston Expo for 2020, it was good to hear him talk about his Expo idea, which I found refreshing and very intriguing. Also, throughout this paper I will refer to him as Jan.

The story Jan told me was that during JFK's presidency, JFK wanted to celebrate the bicentennial of American independence by holding a World's Fair in a historical American city in 1976. The Kennedy family being from Boston implied that Boston should run as a host city. In the running was also Philadelphia, Washington DC, and Miami. The biggest rival was Philadelphia, whose budget over passed that of Boston's. All these proposals and ideas were happening in the 1060's and 70's when "sustainability" wasn't a trend like today. Yet, Jan identified how broken the current model for World Expos was. This events invite different countries and corporations to exhibit in custom made pavilions, wasting millions of dollars on infrastructure and buildings that were neither architecturally interesting, nor functional after the event. For example, Michelin would make a pavilion in the shape of a giant tire. His proposal envisioned using the Expo campus as an extension of the city by having infrastructure and buildings that could be used after the expo, in essence creating a mini-city. The whole concept was also based on innovation and research. There would be several research categories like, medical, educational, urban, transportation, among others. This implied that instead on inviting Japan to build a pavilion that represents Japan, they would be invited to present their technological innovation in high-speed trains so that other countries would learn about the future technologies for a better city. The whole campus would also house around 40,000 people. Visitors would "live" on the Expo grounds, rather than "visit." The idea was to have visitors experience this "city of tomorrow." After the event, the facilities would provide housing for 40,000 local residents, and would have provided innovation to the city of Boston. At the end, the Expo for 1976 was canceled all together due to local and international political difficulties, like the end of the Vietnam war.

What I get from this talk is that at some point, Boston had a great chance of hosting a World Expo, with less resources, and less infrastructure than what we have now. We are a city of innovation, and as such, we should be thinking at a larger scale, how do we step up the image of Boston. Could we hold the 2020 World Expo? Why not? As we show from our proposal, it is not only feasible, but it is also beneficial. Not only can we celebrate the innovation that oozes in Boston's institutions, but we can show an innovation in creating a new sustainable typology for a world-class event, because Boston is a World-class city.

PETER MEAD

DIRECTOR OF BOSTON REDEVELOPMENT AUTHORITY

How many people have been to the restaurants in the waterfront in South Boston? They wouldn't be there if it wasn't for the Big Dig. 40% of the restaurant clients in those wonderful restaurants in Liberty Wharf come from Framingham and beyond. It's people from places like Framingham, Natick, and Wayland that think of the South Boston waterfront as part of their front yard because it's so easy to get in and out of the city form the West, and certainly people from downtown and other places. It has become a very simple commute.

*at Downtown North Association lunch meeting

THOMAS N. O'BRIEN

FOUNDING PARTNER & MANAGING DIRECTOR

Boston is surprisingly a small city given how the rest of the world perceives Boston to be, and Boston faces a couple of challenges. One is to realize how the rest of the world sees us. The borders between Boston and Cambridge, Brookline and Boston don't really matter to the rest of the world. The second challenge is that because the city is so small and compact, when there is a problem it is a solvable problem.

*meeting at HYM Investment Group office
(HYM Investment Group focuses on redevelopment of BROKEN sites in Boston area)

JENNIFER TOUR CHAYES

MANAGING DIRECTOR AT MICROSOFT RESEARCH NEW ENGLAND

When I lobbied for Microsoft to create a research facility in the Boston area, my pitch was based on two things: first, the thriving academic community, both in the areas that conventionally impact technology and in the social sciences; and second, the city's innovative spirit.

*Issue "Why Boston?", Architecture Boston, Boston Society of Architects

JOI ITO

MEDIA LAB DIRECTOR, MIT

Entrepreneurs in Silicon Valley may be international, but they're not good at thinking globally. Silicon Valley has no culture. Have you ever tried to get food in Palo Alto? I don't think Silicon Valley spends a lot of energy on art, culture, and the humanities. When you're building 3Com and [data] switches, all you need is people who sit and focus on bits. But as we get to the World-Wide Web and think about how does social media impact politics, how does it affect fashion, how do we bring museums online — that is much more New York, Boston, and Washington, D.C. There are hopefully some regional advantages.

*Article from Boston.com

EMBRACING A SHIFT:
BOSTON AS THE CITY OF THE FUTURE

BY KIM POLIQUIN

FOUNDING DIRECTOR OF SHIFT BOSTON

There is a growing hunger for change in cities around the world and this desire will prove to be the spark that ignites a new design era. Where will this new epoch take root? Could Boston become the new living, breathing mini-metropolis -- a city of the future? The answer will depend on whether or not our design community is capable of influencing a city-wide shift in thinking.

Can we as designers challenge others to think beyond traditional constraints? How about a free-fall ride in the slot of the John Hancock tower? How about turning the Fort Point Channel into a large swimming pool? How about ziplines from building to building downtown as a new net-zero carbon form of transportation? How about turning the Filene's Basement wreck at Downtown Crossing into a large underwater diving tank?

The ever-expanding global network is opening up new links for collaboration and placing enormous amounts of information at our fingertips. And as social media diversifies us, a shared vision is bringing us together in ways that would not exist without these tools. A new slipstream network is inspiring designers and visionaries worldwide to embrace a common vision that seeks to improve the human urban experience by merging design, ecology and new technology. The desire to make new ideas come to life is bringing individuals, cultures and disciplines together online to share information. This shift in process is producing a new generation of tech-savvy, experimental designers that are on the cusp of igniting a new era in design. This movement will flood our cities with unimaginable new forms of experiential installations, architecture, landscape and infrastructure. Boston's rich history in innovation leadership makes it an ideal testing ground for new design and SHIFTboston is here to fuel the movement. We seek to force this wave of new design through governing bodies and into the community to make Boston a leader once again.

Since initial establishment in 2008, SHIFTboston has been engaging design professionals around the world and capturing design solutions for the future urban environment. We have reached almost every state in the United States and over 40 countries throughout the world. Our commitment to cultivating a new cityscape is inspiring a shift in the Boston community. We encourage others to get on board to join us in this quest.

CONVERSATION WITH **KAIROS SHEN**

CHIEF PLANNER AT THE BOSTON REDEVELOPMENT AUTHORITY

BY RAFAEL LUNA

On Wednesday January 11, Dongwoo Yim and I met with Kairos Shen, Chief Planner at the BRA, where we had a generous discussion about the Boston past, present, and future. The main points that I found interesting where the focus of Boston as a boutique city, centralized development within the core of the city, and the notion that Boston wants to be cosmopolitan, but perhaps not metropolitan.

There's a certain limit or cap to the growth of Boston. As we have seen from the Population Data (Chapter 01), the city has never grown back to it's capacity of 800,000. In fact, Kairos pictured that the city could probably fit around 900,000. So what is keeping us at 600,000? One of the clues suggested by Kairos was the change in population demographics, not the change in population growth. About one in three of the population of Boston are between the age of 20 and 35.

This is an interesting discrepancy between development projects proposed and the condition of the city. Why are there 12 proposals for highrises, where 6 of them are the same size of the Prudential or taller? If the population hasn't grown, where are we going to get extra people to fill these buildings? What will be the proper programing for buildings that size in a city like Boston. Kairos talked about when Copley mall was proposed, it presented the possibility of a new typology for the city. It presented the chance that maybe this could be the new model for hybrid buildings in the city. As we look now, there hasn't been any new similar development. In comparison, these new high-rise projects present the possibility of introducing further dynamic into the city.
Another clue is seeing who's backing up the developments. Vancouver got introduced to new typologies of highrises when developers from Hong Kong imported their model into a western city. But most of the proposals in Boston have not been from foreign developers.

Most of these developments are focused in 5% of the administrative area of Boston. I brought up again the comparison to the land area of Boston being the same as the land area of Paris, yet we only focus on that 5%. This is an inherent issue of the city. The neighborhoods are very distinct, and they seem to act independently from the others. The city has focused in developing the central 5% not because they ignore the rest, but because the other neighborhoods show signs of not wanting to integrate to the core. This leads to the city only developing certain pockets, for example the innovation district in South Boston.

"Metropolis" invokes an image of a faster, denser, more congested environment. For this reason, we have labeled smaller, gradually growing, and more stable cities "Mini-Metropolises," so that their inclusion can minimize the gap existing in the dialogue for urban strategies of future cities.

ROPOLIS

As cities continue to expand and create fields of urbanity, our understanding and definition of cities must reflect the scale and categories of urbanity. Cities like Boston will continue to operate within their own framework, which we have labeled "Mini-Metropolis". Within this framework, there should be an equal understanding of the built environment that the Mini-Metropolis creates.

Throughout this book we have tried to explain the urban conditions that exist within a Mini-Metropolis, taking Boston as our subject of study. Conditions like Manhattan's "culture of congestion," as described by Rem Koolhaas, is one that gets diluted here, and for that same reason we explore the dilution of its architecture. We experimented introducing the idea of

"Pet Architecture" from Japan using pavilions, "Metropolitan Architecture" in our horizontal ring skyscraper, and "Metropolitan Hybrids" with infra-architecture. We dwelled on the idea that a city can be metropolitan without being a "Metropolis." Through this fiction we hope to open to discussion the possibilities for intensification, concentration and metropolitanism that do not yet exist, but can be imagined in the future.

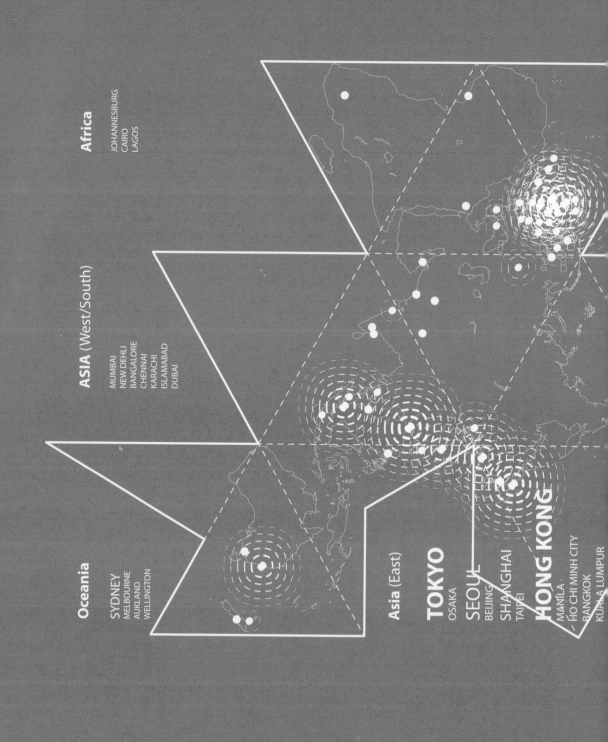

Africa

JOHANNESBURG
CAIRO
LAGOS

ASIA (West/South)

MUMBAI
NEW DEHLI
BANGALORE
CHENNAI
KARACHI
ISLAMABAD
DUBAI

Oceania

SYDNEY
MELBOURNE
AUKLAND
WELLINGTON

Asia (East)

TOKYO
OSAKA
SEOUL
BEIJING
SHANGHAI
TAIPEI
HONG KONG
MANILA
HO CHI MINH CITY
BANGKOK
KUALA LUMPUR

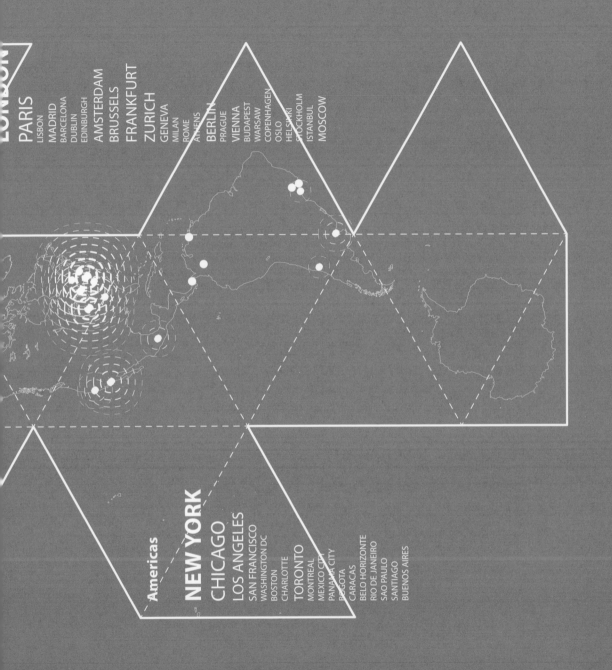

LONDON

PARIS

LISBON
MADRID
BARCELONA
DUBLIN
EDINBURGH

AMSTERDAM
BRUSSELS
FRANKFURT
ZURICH
GENEVA
MILAN
ROME
ATHENS

BERLIN
PRAGUE
VIENNA
BUDAPEST
WARSAW
COPENHAGEN
OSLO
HELSINKI
STOCKHOLM
ISTANBUL
MOSCOW

Americas

NEW YORK
CHICAGO
LOS ANGELES
SAN FRANCISCO
WASHINGTON DC
BOSTON
CHARLOTTE
TORONTO
MONTREAL
MEXICO CITY
PANAMA CITY
BOGOTA
CARACAS
BELO HORIZONTE
RIO DE JANEIRO
SAO PAULO
SANTIAGO
BUENOS AIRES

* INFLUENTIAL CITIES

SELECTED BIBLIOGRAPHY

Blau, Eve and Rupnik, Ivan, *Project Zagreb, Transition as Condition, Strategy, Practice*, Actar, 2007

AECOM, *Asia Beyond Growth*, ORO Editions, 2010

Misselwitz, Philip and Rieniets, Tim, *City of Collision*, Birkhäuser Architecture, 2006

Koolhaas, Rem and Boeri, Stefano, Mutations, *Project on the city*, Actar, 2001

Koolhaas, Rem and Chung, Chuihua Judy, Great Leap Forward / *Harvard Design School Project on the City,* Taschen, 2002

Koolhaas, Rem, *Delirious New York*, The Monacelli Press, 1997

Geipel, Finn and Andi, Giulia, *Grand Paris, Metropole Douce*, Jean-Michel Place, 2009

Susteren ,Arjen Van, *Metropolitan World Atlas*, 010 Publishers, 2004

Fenton, Joseph, *Pamphlet Architecture No.11, Hybrid Buildings*, Princeton Press, 1985

Kaijima, Momoyo and Kuroda, Junzo, *Made in Tokyo*, Kajima Publishing, 2006

Guallart, Vicente, *Sociopolis, Project for a City of the Future*, Actar, 2004

Burdett, Ricky and Sudjic, Deyan, *The Endless City: The Urban Age Project by the London School of Economics and Deutsche Bank's Alfred Herrhausen Society*, Phaidon Press, 2010

Brillembourg, Alfred and Feireiss, Kristin, *Informal City: Caracas Case*, Prestel Publishing, 2005

Atelier Bow-Wow, *Pet Architecture Guide Book, Vol.2,* World Photo Press, 2002

Busquets, Joan, *Cities: X Lines: Approaches to City and Open Territory Design*, Actar D, 2007

Busquets, Joan, *Barcelona: The Urban Evolution of a Compact City*, Actar D, 2006

Berger, Alan, *Drosscape: Wasting Land in Urban America*, Princeton Architectural Press, 2007

IMAGE CREDITS

CREDITS

AUTHORS
DONGWOO YIM
RAFAEL LUNA

EDITORS
DONGWOO YIM
RAFAEL LUNA
CHRISTOPHER GUIGNON
NON ARKARAPRASERTKUL

ILLUSTRATIONS
RAFAEL LUNA
DONGWOO YIM
NEMUEL DEPAULA
EMILY KO
ASHLEY REED
STACY CHOI

GRAPHIC DESIGN
NEMUEL DEPAULA

ACKNOWLEDGEMENT
LINDA JONASH
DUANE LUCIA
PETER MEAD
KIM POLIQUIN
ROBERT O'BRIAN
THOMAS N. O'BRIEN
KAIROS SHEN
RENATA VON TSCHARNER
JAN WAMPLER
CHRISTOPHER WINSHIP

SPONSORS
EUNG HUN BYUN
SE HOON GHIM
DAESIK JUNG
SANG-LEEM LEE(SPACE GROUP)
YOUNGBOON LEE
JINHO MOON (DMP PARTNERS)
DUKE OH
JANET OH
JONG-WON SHIN
MARCUS SPRINGER
DONGSUN YIM
CHANGSOON YOO

PRAUD
Progressive **R**esearch on **A**rchitecture, **U**rbanism and **D**esign

As a research and design firm, PRAUD focuses on a contemporary approach to understanding the effects of urbanity and developing architectural process. PRAUD's research takes into account various scales in architecture and urbanism with key topics such as hybridity, urbanity, density, and transformation. Our architectural dialog is a synthetic gesture between contemporary vocabulary in architecture and urban research.
www.praud.info

Published by
ORO editions
Publishers of Architecture, Art, and Design
Gordon Goff: Publisher
www.oroeditions.com
info@oroeditions.com

Copyright © 2012 by ORO editions
ISBN: 978-1-935935-58-2
10 09 08 07 06 5 4 3 2 1 First edition

Graphic Design: Nemuel DePaula
Edited by: PRAUD
Color Separations and Printing: ORO Group Ltd.
Printed in China.

This book was printed and bound using a variety of sustainable manufacturing processes and materials including soy-based inks, acqueous-based varnish, VOC- and formaldehyde-free glues, and phthalate-free laminations. The text is printed using offset sheetfed lithographic printing process in four color on 120gsm Wood Free paper.

ORO editions makes a continuous effort to minimize the overall carbon footprint of its publications. As part of this goal, ORO editions, in association with Global ReLeaf, arranges to plant trees to replace those used in the manufacturing of the paper produced for its books. Global ReLeaf is an international campaign run by American Forests, one of the world's oldest nonprofit conservation organizations. Global ReLeaf is American Forests' education and action program that helps individuals, organizations, agencies, and corporations improve the local and global environment by planting and caring for trees.

Library of Congress data:

For information on our distribution, please visit our website
www.oroeditions.com